Foolproof Hiring

"I'll tell you straight up—*Foolproof Hiring* is by far the best book I've seen on how to fill your organization with high performers. It's tight, compelling, and research based. You get surprising statistics, captivating stories from Brad and Chris' decades of professional experience, plus a piercing look into the why and how-to of Topgrading. The book is absolutely crammed with the mechanics for epic improvements in how you hire people. *This* is how you build a 5-star organization!"

PRICE PRITCHETT
CEO, Pritchett, LP

"Research shows that most of the people hired in companies are mis-hired, typically costing your company hundreds of thousands to millions of dollars for *each* mis-hire. *Foolproof Hiring* gives you tools and questions to start hiring a lot more superstar A Players (and keep that money to add to the bottom line!)."

EBEN PAGAN
Founder, Go Meta Media; Investor;
Author, *Opportunity: How to Win in Business and Create a Life You Love*

"*Foolproof Hiring* is the easy-to-read and understand reference guide to Topgrading that CEOs have been clamoring for! Hiring A Players is one of the fastest ways to increase your company's profits, and the success and happiness of your existing team. Our company has been using Topgrading, combined with precise rifle-shot recruiting, for the last decade to help our Scaling Up clients achieve a greater than 90 percent A Player hiring success rate. By following the advice in *Foolproof Hiring* and adopting the Topgrading methodology, you can achieve similar results."

RICK CROSSLAND
President, A Player Advantage, LLC

"In order to have the right people doing the right things the right way, we first must hire and onboard well. In *Foolproof Hiring*, Brad and Chris detail the five major hiring problems we're all faced with today, and then provide a practical, easy-to-implement set of solutions and tools to solve these problems and ensure you consistently hire more A Players, more often. It's a must-read for any leader wanting to build a high performing team."

BRAD GILES
Author, *Onboarded: How to Bring New Hires to the Point Where They are Effective, Faster*

"An excellent and timeless resource for CEOs and other leaders of high growth, middle market companies. Getting our people right is critical but not easy. *Foolproof Hiring* has proven tools to significantly improve your hiring effectiveness, and overall approach to managing your talent more strategically."

ETHAN MARTIN,
President and Head Coach, PFD Group, Inc.

"*Foolproof Hiring* is a terrific new book and makes it extremely easy for CEOs and all managers to "test drive" Topgrading. It's like driving a Ferrari for an hour; it doesn't make you an expert, but you just know this is better than an average commuter car. As an Advisor & Coach to CEOs of fast-growing companies, I always recommend Topgrading because when you hire high performers, everything else gets easier."

KEVIN LAWRENCE
CEO, Lawrence & Company Growth Advisors;
Author, *Your Oxygen Mask First*; Key contributor, *Scaling Up:
How a Few Companies Make it... and Why the Rest Don't*

"Topgrading is the foundation of our hiring practices at Advantage Media. Brad Smart and Chris Mursau's new book, *Foolproof Hiring,* brilliantly encapsulates the key concepts that can put your company on the fasttrack to hiring and retaining A Players."

ADAM WITTY
Founder and CEO, Advantage Media

"Hiring is inevitably imperfect, because human judgments are fallible. But it's our conviction at Avenues that Topgrading is the best approach there is for making high-impact hires at all levels, but particularly at senior levels where bad hires are extremely costly. This book gives a clear, accessible explanation of Topgrading while addressing common concerns and misconceptions about hiring practices. Every leader concerned about improving hiring results should read it and try out its recommendations."

DIEGO MERINO
Global Director of Recruitment, Avenues: The World School

"*Foolproof Hiring* gives anyone who needs to fill an open position the tools they need to fill the job with an A Player. Not only do you dramatically increase the chance of hiring the right person, *Foolproof Hiring* shows you how to do it as efficiently as possible."

GEOFF WOODS
Chief Growth Officer, Jindal Steel & Power

"Brad Smart and Chris Mursau are back with *Foolproof Hiring*, an invaluable resource in leveraging Topgrading concepts that produce the best possible hiring results! If you read *Topgrading* and employ those concepts in hiring, you'll love *Foolproof Hiring* as a back-to-basics follow-up; If not, it's a must-read to provide the right tools in hiring A Players."

GEORGE RABLE
Chief Culture and People Officer, Benco Dental

"Brad and Chris nailed it as 'first aid for your hiring ailments.' This is a fantastic book to use as your initial learning about Topgrading or as a boost of learning if you have already been using some of the methods. In particular, the chapter on Applicant Screening Tools was very helpful and we are implementing two of the ideas immediately."

KEVIN RHODES
Founder and CEO, Fragrance Manufacturing Inc.

"At Scaling Up we've coached thousands of entrepreneurs on best practices, and Topgrading has always been one of our pillars. With A Players on their team, all the other Scaling Up methods work better. *Foolproof Hiring* is perfect—a quick read busy CEOs can absorb in a couple of hours and implement right away, to avoid bad hires."

VERNE HARNISH
Founder, Entrepreneurs' Organization (EO);
Author *Scaling Up (Rockefeller Habits 2.0)*

"Topgrading has definitely made two companies I've run more profitable. Nothing has been more important for my career success. Really—at least half my career success is attributable to Topgrading and Brad Smart's counsel."

SCOTT CLAWSON
CEO, Culligan Water

Foolproof Hiring

Foolproof Hiring

Powerful, Proven Keys

to Hiring **HIGH** Performers

Brad Smart
& Chris Mursau

Forbes | Books

Published by Forbes Books, Charleston, South Carolina.
Member of Advantage Media.

Forbes Books is a registered trademark, and the Forbes Books colophon is a trademark of Forbes Media, LLC.

Printed in the United States of America.

10 9 8 7 6 5 4 3 2

ISBN: 979-8-88750-084-3 (Hardcover)
ISBN: 979-8-88750-085-0 (eBook)

LCCN: 2022921661

Cover design by Matthew Morse.
Layout design by Matthew Morse.

Since 1917, Forbes has remained steadfast in its mission to serve as the defining voice of entrepreneurial capitalism. Forbes Books, launched in 2016 through a partnership with Advantage Media, furthers that aim by helping business and thought leaders bring their stories, passion, and knowledge to the forefront in custom books. Opinions expressed by Forbes Books authors are their own. To be considered for publication, please visit **books.Forbes.com**.

We dedicate *Foolproof Hiring* to all past, present, and future Topgraders, so that with more A Players their companies make more money. But on a very personal level, we hope that with your teams of mostly A Players, you enjoy greater career success.

Contents

You Can Hire a *Lot* Better

Talent—or, more accurately, a lack of talent—consistently comes up as one of the top concerns of CEOs, human resources leaders, and talent acquisition managers, and it is definitely on the minds of managers at all levels. Training, development, and succession planning certainly have an impact on the level of talent in an organization, but talent starts with hiring. You need to get the right people in the door, and we know from seventy-five years of combined experience focused on hiring, way too many new hires disappoint. Our research shows that, when analyzed critically, only one in four new hires turns out to be a high performer, a great team player, and a great fit in the company culture.

Bad hires are a recurring nightmare that you don't need to have anymore. In analyzing the hiring processes and hiring results of thousands of companies, we have identified the most serious and chronic hiring problems. We'll address each and tell you about some solutions that have worked in organizations, big and small, for decades. Most of the solutions are simple to understand and can be implemented right away.

We have found that hiring is one of the most broken functions in most organizations—everywhere. How often have you had high expectations for someone you just hired only to find out a few weeks in that they were a mis-hire, either falling short on performance or not fitting your culture, or both? And when unemployment is low, hiring the next warm body can seem necessary just to keep the business running, so the goal of hiring high performers can be thrown out the window.

It would be understandable for you to internalize these hiring mistakes. "Am I a bad interviewer? Am I just terrible at reading people? Why can't I find the right tool to identify great candidates?" The truth is that it's not your fault. You have made hiring mistakes because your hiring methods let you down.

- **Typical hiring processes use recruitment methods that are flawed.** They don't produce enough applicants. A small applicant pool reduces the probability there is even one, let alone multiple, high performers in it.

- **Typical hiring processes use ineffective applicant-screening tools.** Personality tests, artificial intelligence–assisted tools—you name it—all produce pretty charts and graphs, but our research shows that too often they eliminate great candidates, show bias, and let weak candidates through. There are books, articles, and websites that show people how to "game" these screening tools.

- **Typical hiring processes fail to generate candidate candor.** So you really don't know enough about their strengths and not *nearly* enough about their weaker points until after they are hired.

- **Typical hiring processes use shallow interview methods that are unrevealing**, making it easy for any candidate to shine and for low performers to fool you (hence, the title of this book).

- **Typical hiring processes fail to provide reliable verification** of what candidates told you, which is necessary for you to *really* know if the person will turn out to be a great hire or if they will disappoint. Reference calls with friends of candidates, character references, are mostly worthless.

Every hiring method we have analyzed suffers from at least one, and usually many, of these problems, making it virtually impossible to consistently make the right hiring decision. We have spent the past fifty years in search of solutions to the problems and landed on several that have consistently worked well for our clients. Do you see a thread running through these problems? It's lack of honesty—the fundamental problem that mostly accounts for your mis-hires. Topgrading assures honesty and transparency, so you will no longer be fooled into mis-hires. Our solutions make up our methodology—Topgrading—which is also the name of our firm. The methodology has been described, in great detail, in three editions of the book *Topgrading*.

You really *can* improve your hiring results. This book will show you how to attract a lot of applicants, effectively screen in just the best candidates, ensure candidate transparency and honesty, reveal not just candidate strengths but their weaker points, and enable you to always get accurate verification of what candidates say. The "Resources" section will help you get started using the tools and methods you will learn about and present ways to continue your mastery of Topgrading.

Our promise to you is this: using just the methods featured in this book, you will begin hiring more A Players, whether you are a CEO, first-level supervisor, or HR professional. And, yes, there is unprecedented evidence that Topgrading delivers the promised results. We have dozens of documented case studies and hundreds of informal accounts, from Global 100 companies to fast-growing start-ups, that achieved an average of 85 percent success in hiring high performers.

Tens of thousands of managers have accelerated their careers using this process to ensure their teams boast mostly A Players. And Topgrading methods utilize hard, factual candidate information to minimize bias and discrimination.

We've written *Foolproof Hiring* to get you started in your quest to hire better. Think of it as first aid for your hiring ailments. You will learn methods that can produce quick improvements, but, continuing the metaphor, reading this book will not turn you into a "hiring brain surgeon." Some keys, such as in-depth interviewing, require more learning and practice to master. Think about the training necessary to become an EMT versus the education and experience necessary to work as a surgeon; the same principle applies here. Using the solutions in this book to get some quick hiring wins will motivate you and your team to keep learning and practicing the methods. As you continue to improve your hiring success rate, you will achieve a really strong, cohesive team that not only has fun but gets better results.

> We've written *Foolproof Hiring* to get you started in your quest to hire better. Think of it as first aid for your hiring ailments.

All but one (PreScreen Snapshot) of the keys outlined here have been in effect for decades. Some case studies and client quotes generated since Chris and Brad teamed up years ago are included, because there is no "expiration date" for Topgrading, for the one hiring method that ensures greater honesty. Key Topgrading methods were "revolutionary" decades ago and are every bit as valid and effective (and "revolutionary") today. But today, and every day, millions of people are hired, and about half are mis-hired because they "fooled" their employer. We are disappointed that Topgrading methods, despite unprecedented case studies, have not become more widely accepted. *Foolproof Hiring* was written in the hope that the simple methods that produce more honesty in hiring and better performers become "standard."

About the Authors: Learn from the Experts

CEO of Topgrading, Inc., Dr. Brad Smart has often been described as one of the world's leading experts on hiring. Brad has written seven books on hiring, including *Wall Street Journal, New York Times*, and *Amazon* bestsellers. That makes Brad, by far, the most published author on hiring. Although some key Topgrading methods were created in the 1970s, the first book (*Selection Interviewing: A Management Psychologist's Recommended Approach*) was published in 1986. *The Smart Interviewer* and *Topgrading for Sales* followed, and then three editions using the word *Topgrading* in the title were published in 1999 (*Topgrading: How Leading Companies Win by Hiring, Coaching and Keeping the Best People*), 2005 (same title, fully revised second edition), and 2012 (*Topgrading: The Proven Hiring and Promoting Method That Turbocharges Company Performance, third edition*). Each new hiring book—including this one, number seven—reinforces some basics but also explains new ways to make hiring easier and better.

Chris Mursau joined Brad in 2000, and since 2018, he has served as President of Topgrading, Inc., guiding the team that conducts all training sessions and workshops. He has directed training for tens of thousands of managers. Under Chris's direction, our experts have conducted over twenty thousand in-depth assessments of candidates for high-level positions, where the costs of a mis-hire are so high that companies want a second-opinion assessment before making an offer. Chris has headed all recent company-wide Topgrading implementations, resulting in the most recent case studies and quotes by top executives. And Chris, along with Brad's son Geoff (of ghSMART, an executive assessment/coaching firm), has partnered with Brad over the years to fine-tune Topgrading.

We promise to explain simple, proven, "common sense" keys to improve your hiring. But ... those keys start on p. 57. Why don't we *start* with them? The answer is that we've learned from experience that the keys to hiring success require explanations to understand the context in which they are successful. Without that *context* people can easily make incorrect assumptions and fail to get the desired results. For example, the keys will help you hire more A Players ... but "A Player" is a term that is used many different ways, so an early chapter gets us on the same page for the definition. The early chapters also have exercises that, when you do them, will enable you to *experience* a reality rather than just read an opinion.

Do you skim books? Of course you do! So we've done two things in this book to help skimmers:

1. We repeat important concepts with a bit more explanation and practical suggestions for each subsequent mention.
2. Chapter Summaries provide a quick check. Is a bullet point not clear? Go back to learn it.

Learning new disciplines is work but as soon as you experience the promised benefits, you'll be having fun. You can get started Topgrading immediately and experience success in ways you could never imagine. When your hiring activities suddenly change from a series of guessing games to a series of progressively deeper and far more accurate insights into candidates, you will be happy ... excited ... thrilled. Success is fun, right?

CHAPTER 1

Your Hiring Experience Is Disappointing

Those who build great companies understand that the ultimate throttle on growth for any great company is not markets, or technology, or competition, or products. It is one thing above all others: the ability to get and keep enough of the right people.

—Jim Collins, *Good to Great*

We know you are eager to get to the solutions. If you have read one of the previous editions of *Topgrading* or have attended a two-day Topgrading workshop, feel free to skip ahead. If not, read the next two chapters to understand where we're coming from and why the solutions to your hiring problems work. In this chapter, we'll explore:

- A typical hiring scenario,
- Why you are frustrated, and
- What we mean by *high performer* and *A Player*.

The Typical Hiring Scenario

You need to hire a manager. The predecessor's resignation came as a surprise, and your team is left in the lurch.

Most companies work hard to get a lot of résumés to increase the probability that there are A Players in the hiring funnel. For this scenario, let's assume recruitment is good—because if it isn't, if you only have a handful of mediocre and weak applicants, it doesn't matter which hiring methods you use, since your chances of hiring a high performer are slim. Unless you are using excellent, very targeted recruiters, the more applicants you have, the greater the likelihood that there are A Players among the résumés. The next "warm body," or even the best of five applicants, will seldom turn out to be a high performer.

So, you and the team recruited very well—everyone, including you, contacted possible candidates (in their networks) and posted the job on ZipRecruiter, Indeed, and other job boards. Even with high demand for managers in your industry, let's assume fifty people applied, and forty-five of those applicants actually had experience managing a team. It's nice to get so many résumés, but it takes several hours to plow through all of them, trying to figure out with whom you should actually talk. You've read a ton of résumés over the years, and you know (because of your mis-hires) there is serious fiction in many (maybe most) of them—idealized profiles, like those that are portrayed in social media profiles. Unfortunately, often it's a guessing game trying to figure out which résumés might fool you.

So, you use some common screening tools. You ask applicants some knockout questions and require the completion of an intelligence test and an online personality test. Your *applicant tracking system* (ATS) uses *artificial intelligence* (AI) to do a keyword match between the job ad and the résumés you received, eliminating many of your would-be applicants. And you try one of those zillion AI-assisted screening apps that promise to identify A Players. Starting with forty résumés, suppose you eliminated ten with the knockout questions, five more with an intelligence test, and five more with the personality test and AI-tool results. There are twenty left—still too many to phone screen, and the pressure to hire someone is mounting!

You scour the remaining twenty résumés, but it's like trying to read a crystal ball—you just do not know how much hype is in each résumé. You have some confidence that the knockout questions ("Are you willing to work out of the Arctic Circle office?") eliminated the right applicants, but you wonder if you eliminated the right people based on the intelligence and personality test results. So, you stare at the twenty résumés, cross your fingers, and schedule phone screen interviews with candidates who have the best-*looking* résumés.

Phone screen interviews can be frustrating because you know résumés were written to highlight the person for the job *they* want— not necessarily the job you're *filling*. And although everyone has short-comings and weak points, those are never mentioned in résumés and rarely revealed during interviews. You're pretty sure a lot of résumés inflate accomplishments. But *which* résumés? You know you were being fed with rehearsed answers in some phone screen interviews, because some interviewees, when asked for weaker points, turned them into positives. ("I'm obsessed with doing things the right way, so I probably spend too much time double- and triple-checking things.")

Next, the three candidates, who *seemed* best in phone screens, are invited to participate in a round of competency-based interviews (virtual or live). Your company thinks it is using best hiring practices by identifying eight key competencies for the role and asking four coworkers familiar with the job to help out by using standard interview questions that elicit behaviors on those competencies.[1]

In these interviews, you were assigned "technical skills" and "work experience"; the second interviewer asks questions about "decision-making" and "organization"; the third interviewer covers "leadership" and "motivation"; and the fourth interviewer assesses "effective team player" and "culture fit." Candidates are interviewed for about an hour by each of the four interviewers, and all interviewers ask the same questions to each candidate (plus original follow-up questions they think of).

At 4:00 p.m. that day, the interviewers all get together and compare notes. They agree on some strengths but have remarkably different views of the candidates' weaker points. It's like the story of four blindfolded people who each touch a different part of an elephant—midsection (hippo?), trunk (snake?), tail (lizard?), teeth (cow?)—and then try to determine what kind of animal they are touching. They only understand a small piece of the animal and must guess the rest. Your group of interviewers has the same problem. They all heard many positive answers to questions but simply did not learn much about the candidates' weaker points—factors that might result in a hiring mistake, a mis-hire. There is no real consensus. When candidates were asked directly about weaker points, you didn't learn much. You certainly know that the people whom you mis-hired in the past *failed to tell you about their significant weaker points and mistakes*—the ones that made them a mediocre performer or worse; the ones that, had the candidate been more forthcoming, would have convinced you to *not* hire them.

---

1   An example of a behavior-based competency interview: If the competency is "effective team player," a question might be "What are some examples of when you were an effective team player?" or "What are some examples of times you could have been a better team player?"

The data you have on the candidates is just not consistent, and it's full of holes. But you must hire someone, so, alas, you decide on two finalists and call the references they listed—typically friends and associates, who they know will give glowing testimonials.

You wouldn't buy a pre-owned car without checking its maintenance history, and you wouldn't hire a nanny without talking with the parents of the kids they supervised. In business, you don't make a major purchase of equipment without thoroughly analyzing its performance and calculating the ROI. But in a typical hiring process, you lack verification of what candidates told you. You almost never get to talk with managers candidates reported to—the people who best could appraise your finalists.

Many companies skip reference calls altogether because the three "friends" candidates provide as references don't reveal much. Candidates, even A Players, rarely include their bosses in their list of references because everyone knows that *most companies discourage managers from taking reference calls for fear of being sued because a former manager provided a negative review that resulted in the candidate not getting the job.* Though you would love to talk with the finalists' managers, you don't even try to contact them, figuring they wouldn't take your calls. So, you call human resources departments of former employers, confirming just the basics (starting and final dates, job titles, eligibility for rehire), and conduct a basic background check, but those steps don't reveal much more than the company, job title, and dates on their résumé.

You know you need more information, a *lot* more information, but accept the fact that your hiring approach won't produce it. So you press on, fill the job, and hope for the best. The best-*appearing* candidate is hired, but considering so many disappointing hiring results, no one is confident that this person will be a high performer. Within a month or two, you begin to see indications of weaknesses that were not evident during the hiring process, and you "live with" marginal performers and eventually manage just the worst performers out of the organization. In the final analysis, you say to yourself, "The new hire failed because we didn't understand the candidate's weaker points nearly enough."

Adding to your frustration, companies such as ZipRecruiter and Indeed say in ads, every day, that they find passive candidates—people not looking for a job. This is AI-assisted recruiting. However, job seekers have figured out that to be picked by your ATS, all they have to do is change their résumé to use keywords in your ads. (If your ad is for a project manager, they just change some résumé titles to include "Project Manager.") A 2022 *Wall Street Journal* article actually instructs job seekers on how to do this. If a job seeker wants to game the system, there are ample resources available to help them do so.

For companies doing their own recruiting, the Society for Human Resource Management (SHRM) and HR.com present webinars and white papers on hiring, but their advice is all over the place. There are no standard hiring best practices because, bottom line, the actual results of what they teach aren't shown to significantly improve *Quality of Hire*—a problem CEOs are passionate about improving. One way or another, companies must try to get a lot of applicants, but then they must use a screening tool to focus on what they hope are the best candidates. HR managers complain of being inundated with marketing material for products claiming to improve hiring through the use of voice recognition, body language, clues on social media, and machine-learning algorithms purported to predict candidate success. They test-drive the products, find they don't work, and keep trying new ones with similarly disappointing results.

It gets worse. Most companies try but don't get nearly enough applicants because they don't recruit well enough. They don't get a pool of applicants large enough to hire high performers because there may not be *any* high performers who apply. When unemployment is low, hiring managers can be so eager to fill a job that corners are cut during the hiring process, with even shorter, more superficial interviews conducted and no references called. As the new hire is onboarded, you want the person to succeed, and it's natural to be "blinded by the light," overlooking early indications of a mis-hire. After nonperformance has become glaringly obvious, you think back on the hiring process that failed you. You realize that screening tools, tests, interviews, and reference calls all failed to reveal the serious negatives that resulted in the mis-hire—negatives such as not fitting your culture, being fired for poor performance, experiential gaps, poor work ethic ("quiet quitting"), poor work habits, or a poor leadership style. ("My boss was a jerk.") Your optimism usually doesn't last more than a few weeks.

Back to the scenario … You're frustrated and blame yourself, maybe for not asking the right questions, not interpreting answers, being overly sympathetic to a candidate who is desperate to get a job. And maybe, just maybe, you put on rose-colored glasses because you liked the candidate because they attended your alma mater. Additionally, you're upset with the new employee for withholding negative information that would have resulted in you not hiring them.

Bottom line, you are overwhelmed with hiring needs, but flawed methods of hiring haven't worked. What is truly disappointing is that, aside from new-technology products and job boards, all these frustrating problems caused hiring results to be poor fifty years ago, when Brad started his career. Hiring methods have always been problematic, and still are, because the biggest problems have not been systematically solved, except by Topgrading.

Disappointing results are not because you are deficient as a leader. No way. The blame should be directed elsewhere. You are not to blame for so many bad hires—your hiring method is failing you and your company.

> **You are not to blame for so many bad hires—your hiring method is failing you and your company.**

The good news is that the methods you will learn will give you proven, time-tested solutions to all the problems described—the big problems that plague your hiring process. You will definitely hire better by just using the solutions to the major hiring problems you'll read. But if you do the "Recommended Exercises," you can enjoy even better hiring results. And, as promised, you can implement almost all the keys immediately. You will not only hire better; you will almost certainly hire faster, since you will not be wasting time with poor candidates.

We Wrote This Book Because You Deserve Better

Previous editions of *Topgrading* were lengthy and complex. They were the textbooks for companies that were fully implementing Topgrading, supplementing multiday training sessions with coaching by Topgrading professionals throughout the hiring process until managers became comfortable and effective. Trained managers used the methods again and again, getting better and better at interviewing and hiring. The major problems with hiring disappeared, and the "Recommended Exercises" scattered throughout this book became second nature, producing even greater hiring results. Put simply, thousands of managers became hiring and interviewing experts, some qualifying as "hiring surgeons," with the results to prove it.

That being said, we've heard over the years that most people who read a *Topgrading* book do *not* participate in a corporate rollout and can understandably conclude, "Topgrading almost certainly gets better hiring results, but it's so complex I don't know what I, an individual manager, can do." In the absence of thorough training, credible answers, and tons of experience, many or even most managers put the *Topgrading* book on a shelf to gather dust. They never even got started. The 2005 second edition had over six hundred pages. If a manager was trying to use the methods in it on their own without company support, it was probably useful ... as a doorstop.

Since this book is meant to be hiring first aid for any manager or company wanting to improve hiring results quickly, we're presenting the Topgrading methodology in the simplest way so it is easier for managers at every level to implement. For *Foolproof Hiring*, we've sifted through decades of experience, hundreds of case studies, and thousands of testimonials, distilling our hiring books, podcasts, webinars, articles, speeches, blogs, workshops, and newsletters to highlight the essentials you need to get started.

In the third edition of *Topgrading*, our vision was summarized as "Topgrade the world," meaning our goal is for these powerful methods to become the globally accepted standard for hiring. We want you to hire better because we have seen the positive impact better hiring has had on company profits and on the success and happiness of individual managers. This is our legacy, our life's work. We hope that *Foolproof Hiring* proves life-changing to you.

CHAPTER 2

Set the Standard– Hire A Players in Every Job

A small team of A+ Players can run circles around a big team of B and C Players.

—Steve Jobs

W hen CEOs and HR leaders learn that the common Top-grading standard is to hire at least 75 percent high performers, they are usually skeptical, to say the least. That standard seems like a pie-in-the-sky goal, truly impossible. When they realize how the deck has been stacked against them and that just a handful of problems prevent them from hiring better, they become more receptive. They recognize that their disappointing hiring results occur because applicants embellish or flat-out lie on their résumé, continue the fiction in interviews, and get away with it because companies discourage managers from taking reference calls.

Candidates know they can game the system because there is no really good way to verify what they claimed. Then leaders learn about the Topgrading solutions and think, "These make sense." They implement the solutions, see them working, and realize, "It actually *is* realistic to hire mostly A Players." This is the story *Foolproof Hiring* will walk you through.

In the meantime, we're not suggesting that you fire your B Players. Eventually, when you and your team consistently uphold the A Player standard, you'll probably help Bs become As, and you'll find that Bs without potential to become As feel out of place and leave. But we're getting ahead of ourselves ...

Topgrading is all about hiring A Players, so let's add a little more clarity to the terms *A Player*, *B Player*, and *C Player*. Everyone says that they'd love to hire A Players, but when they think about it, a lot of questions come up. *A Player* has different meanings to different people. In some companies, an A Player must show potential for promotion or even the potential to rise to an executive-level role. On the other end of the spectrum, some companies use *A Player* as a blanket pat on the back for all employees who are not on a performance-improvement plan.

Common Questions about the Term "A Player"

- How do you define *A Player, B Player, C Player*?
- Must an A Player be promotable?
- What competencies do A Players exhibit?
- Should I consider hiring people who failed in a job?
- Should I fire B and C Players?
- What are the costs of *not* hiring A Players?
- Can everyone become an A Player?

Definitions of an A Player

A Player definition one: A Players are high performers managers would enthusiastically rehire. In the Topgrading interview (see chapter 5), interviewers ask, "Tell me about the team you inherited. What percent were A Players, high performers you'd enthusiastically rehire; B Players, OK performers you lived with; and C Players, poor performers or disruptive to the culture, or both?" That question conveys enough information for managers, including you, to quickly sort their people into the A, B, and C categories.

One indicator that a candidate has been an A Player is something we discovered decades ago: A Player candidates are happy to arrange reference calls with former managers. From the millions of reference calls that have been conducted (arranged by candidates), clients have consistently reported that the A Players they hired were rated *Excellent* or *Very Good* (using a scale of *Excellent, Very Good, Good, Fair,* and *Poor*) by bosses who, additionally, say they would enthusiastically rehire them. This rating scale is important because, as you'll see, applicants who say bosses would rate them better than *Good* performers (i.e., *Excellent* or *Very Good*) tend to turn out to be A Players in the new job. But if bosses only rate them as *Good*, they rarely turn out to be A Players.

Let that sink in—it's a key to Topgrading.

When candidates are told they will eventually have to arrange reference calls with bosses and then asked how each boss will rate them, their guesses are *very* accurate. They would be nuts to tell you Pat Smith will rate their performance *Excellent* in the call they'll eventually arrange—if they are pretty sure she thought they were only a *Good* performer.

There are a couple of additional criteria that refine the *A Player* definition.

A Player definition two: A Players are in the top 10 percent of talent, *at a compensation level high enough to achieve success.* For example, if one hundred candidates apply for a job paying $70,000 and you hire one of the top ten, the chances are pretty good that the person is an A Player. But there are many reasons someone "in the top 10 percent of applicants" could perform poorly—maybe because the industry is declining, the location is unattractive, the organization culture has a bad reputation, the salary level is too low. Recruiting efforts will likely fail, and you will only have low-performing applicants, even if they are in the top 10 percent.

Greg Alexander coauthored *Topgrading for Sales*, with Brad. Greg had accepted a job as Regional Sales Manager for EMC (subsequently sold to Dell for $40 billion). He had taken over the twelfth of fourteen sales regions and quickly learned there was nothing fundamentally "bad" about the region. No, the fundamental problem was talent. He assessed his sales reps and concluded they were good, but the competition had superior talent. So, Greg looked to Topgrading for the solution. He attended a two-day Topgrading workshop, installed Topgrading methods, coached some B Players to become A Players, replaced over half his team, and—ta-da—had the number one region in only one year. Greg inherited mostly *Good* performers, but in the highly competitive technology space, *Good* was not good enough. He paid average salaries for high tech, but that was too low—his main competitors paid more and got higher performers. At the risk of being absurd to make the point, if you bought an NFL team and cut the pay from millions to, say, $15,000 annually, you would probably have thousands of former jocks trying out just for the thrill of living a dream. But your team would never win a game. The "top 10 percent of talent" for $15,000 salaries in the NFL are not A Players.

So, do your salary surveys, investigate what your competitors are paying, and—when you look at the team (Sales, Marketing, Finance, IT, Operations, etc.) and at the specific job you want to fill—don't be a cheapskate. Hire the "top 10 percent of talent" at a salary level that will enable you to beat the competition.

And keep the Steve Jobs quote in mind: Topgrading companies all find that they need fewer people because one A Player can sometimes outperform two lower performers. Mark Watson, retired CEO of Argo, said, "Argo is more successful as a company because Topgrading has resulted in a higher percentage of A Players, and fewer employees overall. We're finding that we can get excellent results with 20 percent less people if they are A Players. It's better to pay six A Players a bit more than have a team of twelve, with only three A Players, and all paid less." Cass Wheeler, retired CEO of the American Heart Association, wrote *Have a Heart*. A great Topgrader ("Topgrading saves lives"), Wheeler said that not-for-profits mistakenly believe that they must accept B and C Players and pay them less than what for-profit businesses pay, believing, "We're a not-for-profit and can't afford to hire top talent." He says, "Nonsense!" He recommends that not-for-profits Topgrade their organization and pay salaries competitive with private industry but save on salaries by hiring smaller teams of mostly A Players.

A Player definition three: A Players meet all key competencies within a reasonable amount of time and fit your organizational culture well. Before recruiting, you should establish minimum acceptable ratings for *all* key competencies for your open role.

A candidate can fall short of your minimum acceptable rating if you are confident that they will meet it in a reasonable amount of time. They are your *A Potentials*. For example, if it's important for someone to become skilled at a specific software application within six months and you have good training, you can hire that A Potential despite the current skill deficiency.

And you should state how long a new employee must stay to justify hiring them. A super A Player executive who quits within a few weeks is a mis-hire. In retail companies that use Topgrading to hire better cashiers and sales reps, it is typically deemed necessary that a new hire stay six months, minimum. For a software programmer, maybe two years is the minimum, and for a manager, five years.

In addition to believing a candidate will achieve an *Excellent* or *Very Good* rating in key competencies, you must be confident the person exhibits the desired values to *fit the organization's culture.*

What we sometimes hear is "Adam is an A Player technically, but as a leader, he's pretty bad. He makes all the technical decisions for his team, but he's not good at recruiting and selecting people, training them, or coaching; he hires C Players and drives away A Players." No Topgrading company would intentionally hire such a person, and, indeed, they would require massive improvements for Adam to keep that leadership job. Overall, Adam is a C Player who at best could be an A Player only in a narrowly defined technical job.

What if the organization's culture is changing? Candidates should fit the new culture. We sometimes hear "Pat is an A Player but doesn't fit our culture." Wait a minute—maybe the CEO is hiring people like Pat because the current culture of the company is outdated, and the CEO is determined to modernize it. Maybe Pat's not fitting is a good thing—especially if she is a change agent, a positive disruptor who can accelerate the changes the CEO wants. Maybe the board has determined that diversity goals have not been met, so perpetuation of the existing culture is not good enough.

We add "culture fit" to our discussions of A Players because A Players must achieve high-performance standards, exhibit all required competencies in a reasonable amount of time, *and* fit or positively disrupt the organizational culture—or they will be a mis-hire.

Set your goal to hire only A Players and A Potentials, not just B and C Players without A potential.

Recommended Exercise

Pause and take a few minutes to answer this question:

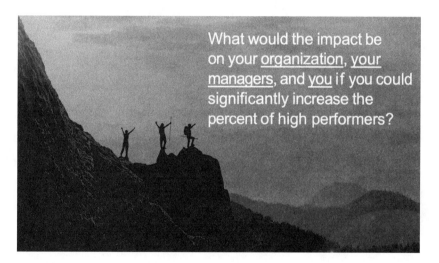

What would the impact be on your <u>organization</u>, <u>your managers</u>, and <u>you</u> if you could significantly increase the percent of high performers?

Some A Players You Hire Must Have the Potential to Be Promoted

Strive to put A Players in all jobs. An A Player sales rep who is not interested in, or likely any good at, leading others is still an A Player sales rep, even though they are not a candidate for VP of Sales. If your company is a start-up or growing rapidly, you'll definitely want to hire some A Players who will be promotable because hiring externally is riskier than promoting from within. You simply know more about internal candidates. Promoting great internal candidates is also good for your organization culture and will help attract more A Players. But

> **Strive to put A Players in all jobs.**

don't force it. Promoting someone just because they perform extremely well in their current role and exhibit your core values could incur the old Peter Principle (promoting people to their level of *incompetence*). The Topgrading methods you will learn for hiring better will also work (with tweaks) for promoting better.

Note that we state *some* A Players must be promotable, but not all of them. We have witnessed some companies, growing fast at first, requiring that *all* new employees be ambitious *and* promotable. Then, when growth slows or inevitable setbacks occur, the A Players were tripping over each other for the next promotion. Every company needs some A Players who are not promotable—high performers who love their job and fit your culture but either do not want broader responsibility or do not have the ability to succeed in a bigger job.

Recommended Exercise

Estimate your talent needs in relation to your growth expectations. How many promotable people should you *now* have to meet your five-year goals? How many will you *have to hire* in order to *mostly* promote from within?

A Player Competencies

What are the typical characteristics of A Players? The following is a partial list of typical competencies A Players in management roles tend to exhibit. They are:

- Smart, intellectual, and business savvy;
- Driven to succeed, passionate;
- Trustworthy, honest;
- Consistent high performers;
- Adaptable, able to adjust to many different personalities;
- Hire almost all high performers;
- Very hard workers;
- Resourceful, overcome obstacles;
- Effective leaders;
- Down-to-earth, grounded, self-aware, humble.

Recommended Exercise

Create your list of competencies, with definitions, for your next open job. Full disclosure: to follow through on this will take more time than it takes you to read this book, so think of this as something high in priority should you decide to learn and apply more than this book's first aid course. Each competency has a thorough definition appropriate for the job. Fifty managerial competencies, with complete definitions, are shown in all six previous Topgrading books. You can draw from these and create competency lists for most jobs. Add your own unique competencies. For a sales rep, maybe fifteen competencies from the list would be needed, with definitions tailored for sales. For a cashier, maybe six competencies will suffice. For jobs with unique requirements, add to or delete from this list.

Here's an example of a competency defined:

Competency: accountability. Holds team members accountable for achieving clearly stated high-performance goals. Confronts nonperformance directly and provides both informal feedback and coaching on a day-to-day basis and in regular performance reviews. Makes it clear that if coaching, training, and effort fail to improve performance to the agreed-upon level, the person will have to either find another job in the company where they can be an A Player or leave the company.

Below is a list of several competencies (sans definitions) that pertain to management jobs:

- **Intellectual competencies:** intelligence, analysis skills, judgment/decision-making, conceptual ability, creativity, strategic skills, pragmatism/problem-solving, risk-taking, business insight.
- **Personal competencies:** integrity, resourcefulness (the most important competency), results orientation, excellence, organization/planning, independence, stress management, self-awareness, adaptability/maturity, self-development.
- **Interpersonal competencies:** first impression, likability, listening, customer focus, team player, assertiveness, communications (oral and written), politically savvy, negotiation skills, persuasiveness.
- **Management competencies:** recruiting/selecting A Players, training/development/coaching, accountability, goal setting, empowerment, performance management, redeploying B/C Players, team building, diversity.
- **Leadership competencies:** vision, change leadership, inspiring followership, conflict management.
- **Motivational competencies:** energy/drive/passion, career ambition, compatibility of needs (with our organizational culture), tenacity, balance in life.

Leaders we've trained have asked, "Can't we cut the list down?"

For nonmanagement positions, we, of course, delete leadership and management competencies. Then we say, "Let's think about an executive-level role and try to shorten the list. Please start by suggesting one we can delete from the list. In which of these competencies can an executive be only *Fair* or *Poor* and still be considered an A Player?"

Crickets. Silence. It's possible that even an executive can be only *Good* in a couple of the competencies and still qualify as an A Player, but that usually means someone else on the team must be *Very Good* or *Excellent* in that area to compensate. The realization that all fifty competencies are not just desirable but necessary initially takes managers aback. To accurately rate a candidate on so many competencies seems impossible. It's not—you'll see.

A Players Are Resourceful

Resourcefulness is the über-competency, an example in which one competency requires strength in a bunch of others. Resourcefulness includes initiative, drive to succeed, independence, and creativity. Resourceful people don't accept setbacks without *passionately trying to figure out how to get over, through, or around barriers to success.* They are strong, determined, effective at making decisions under pressure, willing to take calculated risks, able to get the most from others, inspiring, determined to succeed, tough but fair with people, and fanatically determined to succeed the right way. They don't give up. Did we mention they are driven to succeed?

When the pandemic hit in 2020, millions of people were devastated, and even many ordinarily resourceful people initially experienced anxiety and depression … and career setbacks. After the shock wore off, their resourcefulness kicked back in. They did not complain, hide, panic, or blame others or bad luck. They took some deep breaths and mobilized themselves and others to enable their organizations to survive and maybe even flourish, or at least beat the competition. With businesses unable to survive, even highly resourceful people were let go, and many remained unemployed for a while, persevering until they found jobs. Resourceful managers got creative and made heroic efforts to inspire and appreciate their people, many of whom found their lives shaken to the core.

At the risk of stating the obvious, Topgraded companies survive and can flourish in bad times because they have so many A Players, all of whom are resourceful. They feed off each other; when setbacks occur, their confidence, their can-do attitude, is contagious. Without a critical mass of resourceful A Players, the team's lack of resourcefulness is unfortunately contagious.

As you interview people for professional and managerial jobs, view every response within the framework of "Does this response show resourcefulness?" When interviewing people, constantly look at their career from the vantage point of "Is there a pattern of success, of achieving and exceeding goals, and of overcoming failures, setbacks?" If you rate the person on all competencies for the job, when the ratings are high in the components of *Resourcefulness*, then when you get to rating *Resourcefulness* you'll think, "Yes, this candidate is very strong in the most important competency."

Yes, Consider Hiring Someone Who Has Failed

But be careful.

We have interviewed thousands of candidates for executive positions, and 80 percent of those who were rated A Players and recommended for hire had experienced a *significant failure earlier in their career*. They were a C Player in at least one job. They dusted themselves off, learned from their mistakes, found a new job that was a better fit at that point in their career, and rose to become an A Player in subsequent jobs.

Everyone Can Be an A Player ... Though Not Necessarily in the Job They Want

You know from life experience that some people lack self-awareness and overestimate their abilities and potentials. Sure, we love the movies and stories of how people wouldn't give up their dream, despite failures and discouraging words from others, and they eventually succeeded. Think of the Williams sisters and the hurdles they had to get over in the white, male tennis world. Chris does podcasts with CEOs who pulled themselves out of business and personal setbacks, and their examples are inspiring. The common threads running through their stories are of resourcefulness and determination, of course, but also having the *courage to recognize and fix shortcomings, to "rewire" themselves.* You know of leaders who, the higher they move up careerwise, lose self-awareness, surround themselves with yes-people, and make awful decisions.

We had the honor of designing an emotional intelligence program for a *Fortune* 500 company. The CEO had a gut-wrenching revelation: he was wrong to encourage harsh, top-down, autocratic leadership. One of his not-so-heartwarming mantras was "Leadership is demonstrated when the ability to inflict pain is confirmed." Brings tears to your eyes, right? Coaching sessions were hard-hitting, convincing him to change. He did change, and he required thousands of leaders, who had been doing things such as publicly embarrassing subordinates, to change too. Kudos to a CEO who fixed a major problem in his dealing with people, and kudos to thousands of his leaders who improved from *Poor/Fair* in *Emotional Intelligence* to an average of *Good/Very Good*.

Recommended Exercise

Analyze *why* some of your people are falling short. Are they simply weak on key competencies? Or might there be other reasons, including factors you can influence?

In our experience, most companies have at least a few people who are not performing very well but could become A Players.

There are many reasons why a potential A Player may perform as a B or C Player. Is a Potential A "stuck"? Are they in a job that they are not passionate about, and have they been discouraged from moving to a different job? Are their performance accountabilities unclear? The performance bar must be clearly set at an A Player level and communicated to everyone, but particularly to someone who is not performing. Does a C Player manager stifle them? C Player managers are threatened by A Potential direct reports—those "hard-to-manage upstarts," who are always coming up with ideas for change. Replacing a C Player manager with an A Player can unleash the talents of "underperformers." Is prejudice/bias stifling them? The CEO must take responsibility to reduce such barriers.

How to Handle Underperformers

Do you have several on your team who definitely fall short? Here are the steps managers have taken to move up to A Player status:

- **Topgrade. Implement what you learn in this book.** OK, roll your eyes. Of course, we'll list this first. But frankly, having assessed, coached, and trained thousands of managers in these methods, we are certain that converting teams of 25 percent high performers to teams of 75 percent-plus performers is the surest way an individual manager (you?) can qualify as an A Player. Be like Greg Alexander. Even some of the famous billionaires you've read about, early in their careers, qualified as C Players—but made up for their shortcomings by building strong teams that produced the outstanding results that made their companies highly successful.

- **Get them training and coaching to perform better.** Setting the A Player standard raises the performance bar, and, therefore, much more thorough training and coaching are typically offered to help people become—and remain—A Players. Everyone is happy when people rise to the occasion and perform better. Some of those people, thought to be Bs or even Cs, *ask for training and coaching*, get it, and actually rise to A Player status.

- **Consider job changes for them.** Suppose you have a B Player who, despite coaching and training, is not going to become an A Player in their current role. Seriously consider if they could be an A Player in a different role—a job where they will be more passionate, more driven, and more successful. Kevin Silva, VP Human Resources at Argo, said, "Topgrading methods have enabled us to put B and even some C Players in different jobs where they became A Players." It might be a lateral move into a different area or a move into a narrower job. When a company grows rapidly, the company will naturally outgrow some people. Suppose your Vice President Sales and Marketing was an A Player but sank to a B Player by the time the company doubled in revenue. With greater strength in sales than marketing, that VP Sales and Marketing might be assigned a narrower role—VP Sales—and A Player performance returns.

Although demoting someone with the expectation that they will perform as an A Player in a lower role is not always an option, particularly if it involves taking a salary cut, consider it if the person enthusiastically *embraces* the lower role. H-E-B Grocery Company is the most respected grocery company in the US, when rated by grocery CEOs. The company found that some district managers anticipating retirement were happy to step back to being store managers for a couple of years, for less pressure before retiring. But this is the exception. If someone is realistically over their head, and training and coaching do not result in their achieving A Player results,

> They could be an A Player in a different role—a job where they will be more passionate, more driven, and more successful.

they should not wait for the company to act (and maybe fire them). They should understand that they will not be permitted to remain in that role. They should maybe offer to take a demotion or find a job outside the company that suits them better.

We've worked with a lot of entrepreneurs, and it's very common that start-ups outgrow the founder. Company founders tend to be creative and impatient. They are great at launching ideas early on, but as the company grows, their idea-a-minute approach becomes a burden to those working to execute, and they lack the patience to implement complex operations. Coaching might persuade them to pass the baton to a COO, to free them up to continue originating ideas (which the COO moderates and executes).

Human Resources Leaders Who Improve Quality of Hire Are Almost Always Considered A Players

Topgrading has been key to my career success. I don't know many HR professionals who have achieved anything close to the percent high performers hired that we've achieved at Culligan.

—Gary Parkinson, CHRO, Culligan Water

When an HR leader can document better hiring methods that lead to more A Players hired, they earn respect from the CEO, their peers, and their team. This leads to greater career success for them. CEOs everywhere value HR résumés with accomplishments that include improved talent. We guess only 1 percent of HR professionals have in their résumé something like "Received the President's Award for *Significantly Improving Quality of Hire.*"

HR managers who do not lead Topgrading can still earn promotions by becoming known for being excellent at identifying candidates who, when hired, turn out to be A Players. We typically train HR first so they can show the organization they are key drivers of the new methodology and that they are committed to helping every hiring manager hire more A Players. And in most Topgrading companies, one or two HR professionals become so good at conducting Topgrading Interviews (which you will learn about in chapter 5) that they become the internal resource, partnering with hiring managers conducting interviews. These HR professionals become the primary interviewers, asking the most questions and getting the most credit for filling jobs with A Players—and for identifying those candidates who would most likely turn out to be mis-hires.

Picture this as an HR manager: Using the methods described in later chapters, you convince a hiring manager not to hire their favorite candidate, X. Instead they hire Y, the candidate you predict will be an A Player in the role, and Y indeed turns out to be an A Player. Two months after Y is hired, the hiring manager says, "Thank you! In retrospect, X would have been a very expensive mis-hire!" The respect HR gets—the respect they *earn*—for brilliant hiring insights changes their career for the better. We know many HR professionals who have tripled their salary—a tangible result of earned respect.

A very important point to note is that it's CEOs, *not* human resources, who must drive and be perceived as the driver of A Player job standards and the more systematic, thorough Topgrading hiring methods. HR does the heavy lifting and gets most of the credit, but everyone in the company must know that HR has 100 percent CEO support. It is nearly impossible for HR to uphold the A Player standard without that.

If the CEO delegates the setting of performance standards to HR, HR is hung out to dry! Imagine higher performance standards are rolled out, and HR is emphasizing them in executive talent meetings. The head of Marketing says to the CEO that A Player standards cause too much stress, so he wants to keep the lower standards. He wants to give C Players second and third chances. If the CEO agrees, the A Player standard is dead; HR is thrown under the bus. HR has to be able to say to a peer who is trying to cut corners or undercut the A Player standards, "The CEO is adamant about the higher standards—so, no, we won't reduce your team's performance targets."

Set the A Player Standard ... and Fire Bs and Cs? No, You May Not Have to Fire Anyone!

When our clients set, reinforce, and enforce A Player standards, they rarely have to fire people. Why? Those who chronically underperform—even after training, coaching, and considering job changes—know that they cannot continue to fall short of their performance accountabilities and keep their job. Chronic low performers, who do not improve sufficiently with training and coaching or move into a job where they can perform well, typically leave voluntarily. It's a lot easier to get a job when you have a job. So, when an underperformer quits, host a last lunch, have a cake, and wish them well.

The Clawson brothers, Curt and Scott, are good examples of how to manage B and C Players. Curt was CEO of the world's largest wheels manufacturer (Maxion) and then a congressman. Scott is the super successful CEO of Culligan Water. Both are excellent at upholding the A Player standard. (You can read their case studies at Topgrading.com.)

During the pandemic and Great Resignation, one of the main reasons people changed jobs was because they did not like or respect their manager, feeling that they were unfairly treated. The *Wall Street Journal* reported a survey showing over 70 percent of people who quit their jobs considered their boss "a jerk." (Think of all the mis-hired leaders who were jerks.) The methods outlined in this book will result in a deep understanding of a candidate's leadership style and how well a candidate will fit the culture you want to have.

To minimize turnover and voluntary turnover due to frustration with managers, the Clawson style is to ...

- **Hold people accountable for hiring A Players.** So, there will be very few mis-hires, and almost all managers hired are trusted and respected by their teams.
- **Create solid, fair job scorecards** (see "Hiring Solution #1"), with measurable accountabilities, at the beginning of the recruitment process. Too often hiring is done based on vague job descriptions. Job scorecards help you avoid mis-hires because candidates, and the managers they serve, are clear about expected performance and behaviors.
- **Provide every employee with regular performance feedback and coaching, starting with onboarding.** Everyone should create and be working on an individual development plan. This probably sounds bureaucratic to small-company managers, but everyone needs to know how their performance is judged. If you create a job scorecard, you have the foundation for performance appraisals. With a solid performance management system, it becomes clear if someone is falling short. In that case, an aggressive training and coaching program is launched. Again, the job scorecard is the basis for performance appraisals, and if someone is falling short, you owe it to them and the company to give them feedback, training, and coaching.
- **Take into consideration personal issues, health problems, and other extenuating circumstances.** They allow for mistakes. Risks are taken in a high-performance culture, and to not stifle creativity, mistakes are analyzed, fixes are implemented, and

ways to prevent similar mistakes are embraced. And then it's "Move on!"

- **Look for internal opportunities in a different role where the person can be an A Player if they continue to fall short in their current job.** But when all else fails and the person quits, have a nice lunch for the departing employee.

To the Clawson brothers, these steps have become natural, "obvious," and common sense.

Chapter Summary

- A Players are people you would enthusiastically rehire.
- Hire enough promotable As to mostly promote from within (rather than hiring externally).
- Most A Player executives have failed in a job (and learned from the failure).
- Almost all great HR managers who improve Quality of Hire are A Players.
- CEOs must empower HR to uphold A Player standards.
- Set the A Player standard, hold people accountable to achieve it, and let people know they cannot keep their job if they fail. Underperformers will quit rather than wait to be fired.

CHAPTER 3

Measure Your Hiring Results

Historically, we measured nearly everything. Yet, until we embraced the Topgrading philosophy and tools, we never measured how well we hired. And we never estimated costs of mis-hires and that's a real eye-opener.

Now, measuring costs of not Topgrading and success with Topgrading we see the results on the bottom line. E*TRADE would have failed, but Topgrading helped me turn it around.

—Paul Idzik, CEO (retired)

Every company that values talent must measure hiring success. When we started Topgrading we did the measurements and estimated the percent of our employees who were A Players. Our percent of A Players has improved—95 percent of our employees are A Players and it has made a huge difference in employee satisfaction, employee engagement, and most importantly, the bottom line. Measuring hiring success keeps us focused on achieving 95 percent success. We are now one of Utah's fastest-growing companies.

—Travis Isaacson, Sr. Director Organization
Development, Access Development

W e're looking for a metaphor … You're the emperor, and we have to point out that you're probably not wearing clothes. Or … Failure to measure hiring results is the huge elephant in the room. Peter Drucker, one of the greatest leadership gurus of the twentieth century said, "The ability to make good decisions about people represents one of the last reliable sources of competitive advantage, since very few organizations are very good at it."

> The only acceptable hires are A Players and A Potentials (people who are not yet A Players but who, with experience and training, are "getting there"). Everyone short of that is a mis-hire.

You measure everything else that is important in your business. With your goal of improving talent, rigorously tracking costs of hiring mistakes (what we refer to as *mis-hires*) and what percent of your hires turn out to be high performers will reinforce your commitment to continue using the methods recommended in this book.

A reminder: Our perspective, and the perspective of our clients, is that when Topgrading is implemented, the only acceptable hires are

A Players and A Potentials (people who are not yet A Players but who, with experience and training, are "getting there"). Everyone short of that is a mis-hire.

Calculate the Costs of Hiring Mistakes

We've researched the costs of hiring mistakes by taking thousands of managers through a short exercise. We asked managers to think of a specific non-A Player they have worked with and estimate costs in the following categories:

1. Hiring costs
2. Compensation (base, bonus, commission, benefits, etc.)
3. Cost of maintaining the person in the job (office, car, executive assistant, computer, etc.)
4. Severance
5. Cost of mistakes, failures, wasted and missed business opportunities
6. Disruption

The first four categories are the "hard" costs and are easy to jot down. Number five takes a bit more thought, and here is a simple way to think about it: What results did you expect an A Player in the role to deliver? What did the B or C Player actually deliver? And what were the financial costs of the differential between your expectations and the actual results?

Number six, disruption, is often the most underestimated area. It is challenging to put a specific number on things like lower morale or lower productivity from A Players who are covering for non-As. But try—think of how your low-performing manager negatively impacted their team's results, your results, and their peers' results.

When the managers were simply asked to estimate the total costs when they mis-hired a specific person, the estimate is high. But when entire teams think of a clear mis-hire, the costs are typically much higher.

Recommended Exercise

Use the Topgrading "True Costs of a Bad Hire" calculator. Use it to measure costs of mis-hires. It's free at https://topgrading.com/resources/mis-hire-calculator/.

After being surprised at *their* cost estimates, any team becomes more convinced of the value of replacing their current hiring system. Here are the averages of our research over the years:

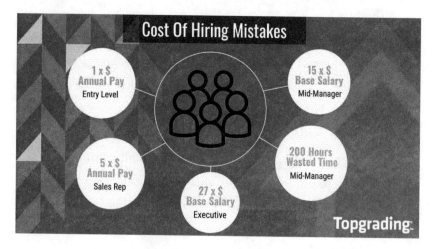

This chart shows financial costs that hiring mistakes cause, but our Topgrading "True Costs of a Bad Hire" calculator also suggests that you estimate the hours "wasted" (by you and others) preventing and fixing mistakes by low performers. "Wasted" is in quotation marks because when you're preventing or fixing problems an A Player would have avoided, those hours are *necessarily* spent. They are not really wasted, but you get the point. When a management team adds up their individual estimates of time spent to prevent and fix problems caused by Charlie (especially categories five and six above), it's hundreds of hours for a mid-manager and thousands for all the time lost because of a mis-hired executive.

A few years ago, *Chief Executive* magazine, in a cover story on the cost of mis-hires, used our calculator to arrive at the cost of a mis-hired CEO to be 27 × base salary (27 × $500,000 = $13.5 million). The article pointed out that when CEOs are forced to resign, successors typically bring in their team, so there are big costs in replacing C-suite executives—nudging out the former team and bringing in an entire new team. *Harvard Business Review* noted, "80 percent of employee turnover is the result of bad hiring decisions." According to a study conducted by Link Humans and reported by *Undercover Recruiter*, for a second-level manager (employed at an organization of any size) who earns $62,000 per year and has been terminated after two-and-a-half years, the bottom-line costs to a company over thirty months are $840,000.

Measure Your Hiring Success

(This is not a "Recommended Exercise"; doing this is probably essential for you to emotionally commit to embracing Topgrading.) You'll get a very uncomfortable feeling in the pit of your stomach when you begin to add up the costs, but this will motivate you to do a better job the next time you need to fill an open position.

When asking CEOs and HR heads why they don't measure hiring success, a common excuse is "We're all overwhelmed and can't take the time to measure and track hiring success." One company you know well was asked by the American Productivity & Quality Center (APQC) "What percent of managers you've hired in recent years have turned out to be the high performers you hoped for, expected, and paid for, if the only other category is a mis-hire? If you didn't get the high level of performance you paid for, that's a mis-hire, right?"

The chief human resources officer said his company's success was 97 percent. Wow! That's impressive!

Then APQC asked, "How do you measure Quality of Hire at your company?"

You won't believe the response: "We send the hiring manager an email thirty days after the person was hired asking one yes/no question: 'Does the person you hired thirty days ago have skills to do the job?'"

You read that correctly. The CEO dashboard has that stat, which is about as feeble as asking "Does the person you hired thirty days ago know where to park?" The email is too soon for accurate measurement (thirty days) and doesn't even ask how good the new hire's performance has been. Our hunch is that no one, CEOs and HR included, wants to seriously measure Quality of Hire because the results are so disappointing.

The real reason companies don't measure hiring success is because of the elephant in the room. That huge animal is there for everyone to see and smell, but psychologically it's too hard to face. Companies are so bad at hiring that collectively they are most comfortable making excuses—"People are not widgets; they are complex and unmeasurable" or something like that. CEOs have always told us versions of "Yeah, we suck at hiring, and every CEO I know says their company sucks at hiring. And we just give up, live with policies and procedures that produce mediocre results, and basically ignore the elephant in the room."

Typical Hiring Results

Our research over the decades shows that most managers and companies that use typical hiring methods experience disappointment with at least half of their hires. So, you're probably in good company, suffering along with the vast majority of managers and companies. The question is, How does that make you feel? How much of a burden does it put on you if half of your new employees fall short of your performance expectations and behave in ways that are not in alignment with your company's core values? How do you feel when your new hire makes life difficult for members of your team—so much so that they drain energy from the high performers who must prevent and fix problems caused by the new hire? How do you feel when you realize that—despite your never-ending efforts to salvage chronic low performers—as a group, they have detracted from *your* performance, *your* career success?

To put "candidates fooling you" in perspective, we believe that most people are honest most of the time, but in most countries it is socially acceptable to fudge the truth to get a job. Your mis-hires do *not* occur because you're easily fooled or you're an ineffective interviewer or leader. You probably entered your first leadership position with no training on how to interview or hire. And you are not a professional interviewer; you have leadership responsibilities, and hiring probably takes about 10 percent of your time. With a dizzying array of employment tests, screening tools, and interview questions, how in the world can you be an informed buyer of hiring solutions? You probably haven't read more than one book on hiring or attended more than one short seminar on the subject. So how can you, or any manager, become really good at hiring? This book helps you remove those reasons—those legitimate excuses—for hiring failures.

Peter Cappelli, in a widely read *Harvard Business Review* article, "Your Approach to Hiring Is All Wrong," said, "Only about a third of US companies report that they monitor whether their hiring practices lead to good employees; few of them do so carefully, and only a minority even track cost per hire and time to hire. Imagine if the CEO asked how an advertising campaign had gone, and the response was, 'We have a good idea how long it took to roll out and what it cost, but we haven't looked to see whether we're selling more.'" In our decades of experience, only Topgrading companies measure percent of high performers hired.

CEOs and prominent leadership thinkers believe that talent is an extremely important factor in contributing to the success of any organization. It's the high performers, the A Players at every level of compensation, who make the difference between mediocre and high-performing organizations. A common mantra is "The top 20 percent produce 80 percent of the favorable results."

Recommended Exercise

Calculate your hiring success rate. We define *hiring success* as "filling an open position with an A Player." What percent of the time when you hire someone do they turn out to be an A Player, someone you would enthusiastically rehire? At an organizational level, it's important to measure percent A Players hired. But let's start with you. Your estimated percent A Players hired is your baseline.

Think about the people you have hired over the past two to three years. How many of those new hires turned out to be high performers, fit your culture, and exhibit your core values? And it goes without saying that to qualify as an A Player, a person must stay long enough to deliver great results. Super talented people who quit before they have performed at a level to justify their pay are not A Players.

Recommended Exercise

Estimate how many A Players *you* have on your team. This is different from the exercise above. Theoretically, if you only hire A Players 50 percent of the time but keep firing non-A Players and hiring replacements, you could end up with mostly As on your team. But what a bloodbath of hiring and firing ... and hiring and firing! Just ask yourself which people you would *enthusiastically* rehire—that's a pretty good rough guess as to how many A Players you have.

Our research over the past forty-plus years shows typical hiring results at organizations large and small across the globe are broken down as follows:

Companies use a broad range of rating scales for performance. "Meets" or "Exceeds" or "Fails to Meet" performance goals are common. Another scale is "Excellent Performer, Very Good, Good, Fair, Poor." And there are "A Player, B Player, C Player" designations. Another system rates how enthusiastic a manager might be to rehire someone – "Excellent," "Very Good," etc.

Is Your Hiring 75, 50, or 25 Percent Successful?

Let's pause for a minute and consider the following:

- If your standard is to accept high performers, good performers, and even fair performers as "good enough," you feel 75 percent successful at hiring people.
- If only high and good performers are "good enough," but not fair or poor performers, you feel 50 percent successful.
- If your goal is to hire only *high performers*, A Players, you consider your hiring results only 25 percent successful, since 75 percent of your hires fall short of your high performer standard.

Having worked with hundreds of leading companies and fast-growing start-ups, we know that CEOs, HR professionals, and almost every hiring manager all *want* to hire high performers in every job. But, before using Topgrading methods and tools, most companies and most managers consider themselves about 50 percent successful, with good performers considered "good enough." Please keep an open mind, and think that maybe, just maybe, you can improve your hiring technique and realistically strive to hire people who are better than "good performers," only considering a hire successful if they turn out to be a high performer.

Are Good Performers Good Enough?

Good is the enemy of great. And that is one of the key reasons why we have so little that becomes great. We don't have great schools, principally because we have good schools. We don't have great government, principally because we have good government. And we don't have many great companies, because they lack enough great employees.

—Jim Collins, *Good to Great*

You might ask, "Doesn't every company need people who do good work, exhibit core values, and are great team players but might not be promotable—people like cashiers in a retail store or mid-level managers who lead teams of entry-level personnel who keep the warehouses operating?" Of course! The best organizations strive to hire the best people at all levels, including A Player cashiers who easily engage customers, are highly productive and responsible, and are always on time. To be clear, every great company needs some A Players who have high potential, are promotable, and are on their succession plan. They also need lots of A Players at every level who they can count on to deliver results but who might never rise in the organization or want promotions.

Suppose that of ten finalist candidates for an open cashier job, only one would turn out to be a high performer, three good, three fair, and three poor, all at the same compensation. Why would you not simply hire that one best candidate? If you could identify the high performer, of course you'd hire that person. But because identifying that A Player in the group hasn't been easy, almost all managers identify high-performing candidates only one-quarter of the time!

49

Companies that hire only 25 percent A Players are smart to live with Bs and only replace Cs. Here's why: With only one out of four people hired turning out to be a high performer, trying to replace a poor performer with a high performer is too difficult, too disruptive. Most companies are happy when replacements of C Players turn out to be B Players—hiring a B Player is an improvement. To hold out for an A Player replacement means to hire and then fire one, hire and then fire the second, hire and then fire the third, and *finally* hire an A Player! That is not realistic because it would be terrible for the culture. So, you live with a lot of employees whose performance is disappointing because your hiring method regrettably makes that acceptance rational and smart … until you embrace a hiring method that can consistently get you 75 percent-plus high performers.

The 2020 Conference Board survey (conducted just before the COVID-19 pandemic) showed the #1 concern of global executives was talent—they experience too many bad hires. Unless you are way, way above average, your hiring results disappoint you at least half the time.

What Evidence Exists That Topgrading Is the Most Effective Hiring Method?

You are smart to ask perhaps the most relevant, revealing, and important question to ask if you want a better hiring method: "What evidence should I consider to determine if I should replace my hiring method?" The answer, we suggest, is case studies—documented hiring results with companies and CEOs named, people who you can call for verification.

It's unseemly to brag, but we've learned over the years that companies are very interested in improving their hiring results and really want to know what evidence exists for one method over another.

Companies in the hiring business cite their case studies, so please check them—and us—out. To read our case studies, go to https://topgrading.com/client-results/ or go to "Client Results" by scanning the following QR code:

Other hiring vendors rarely give the name of the company, CEO, or head of HR, sometimes claiming, "All our client information is confidential." Our clients have approved every word in their case studies, and the CEOs attest to the accuracy of the information. Topgrading CEOs and heads of HR were told that academic research would vet their case studies, so they should be prepared to describe the rigor and integrity of their measurements and ratings. Dr. Michael Lorence did just that.[2]

Topgrading companies do brag about their hiring results because it helps them attract and retain A Players. A Players want to work with A Players for obvious reasons—a company with mostly A Players is apt to grow and provide more career opportunities than a typical company with only 25 percent A Players. A Players enjoy teamwork, with teams of A Players. A Players are not happy working with low performers, because they have to spend so much time preventing low

---

2   Michael S. Lorence, PhD, "The Impact of Systematically Hiring Top Talent: A Study of Topgrading as a Rigorous Employee Selection Bundle" (EDB diss., Georgia State University, 2014), https://doi.org/10.57709/5562534. Note: the "bundle" refers to twelve Topgrading hiring methods, not just the four explained in this book.

performers from making mistakes—and as much time fixing their mistakes. The Great Resignation shocked the business world, with employee turnover at record highs—but Topgrading companies had excellent retention, in part because the CEOs built cultures in which people who perform well are celebrated and paid well.

Here is a summary of the hiring results experienced by dozens of documented case studies whereby CEOs and heads of HR vouch for the published results:

Percent High Performers Hired

26%

Before Topgrading

85%

With Topgrading

The average case-study company improved from 26 percent high performers hired prior to Topgrading to 85 percent high performers hired since the Topgrading methodology was implemented. Something else is unprecedented in our case studies: CEOs state, in their own words, their belief that upholding the A Player standard and implementing a much more effective hiring process made the company more successful and more profitable. We are unaware of any other hiring company with even one case study highlighting a fraction of these hiring results or quoting even one such testimonial by a CEO. We are constantly updating and adding to our case studies, and even the older studies are still relevant. Topgrading methods do not have an expiration date; they work as well today (with improvements) as they did forty years ago.

Our Topgrading meeting with top HR executives. We were hired to meet for a day with just the heads of human resources of the top one hundred companies with the highest revenues in the world—the Global 100. We began the day by asking about their hiring goal, which was agreed to be hiring *high* performers. Then all were asked to write down their answer to "What percent of the people you've hired in recent years have turned out to be A Players, high performers, if the only other category is a mis-hire, someone you would not enthusiastically rehire?" This elite group of HR professionals said only 20 percent of the people they hired in recent years turned out to be high performers. Does that surprise you?

That 20 percent included twelve Topgrading companies in the room who reported 80 percent high performers hired. During the day, the Topgraders shared *how* they more than tripled their success hiring the high performers their CEOs expected. Four of the keys to their success that they cited are chapters in this book.

During that meeting, the Global 100 heads of HR were asked "Is there any other hiring approach producing anything close to 85 percent high performers hired?" No hands went up. "Does any method you know of produce even 50 percent high performers hired?" No hands went up. We believe it is because no other hiring method includes solutions to major hiring problems.

> Topgrading methods do not have an expiration date; they work as well today (with improvements) as they did forty years ago.

A final indicator. The APQC conducted a two-and-a-half-year study of Quality of Hire focusing on the best hiring practices of twenty leading companies. There were plenty of innovative practices mentioned, but when it came to actual Quality of Hire, only two organizations (out of twenty)—Lincoln Financial Group and American Heart Association—reported 75 percent-plus high performers hired, and both utilized Topgrading hiring methods.

What would your life and career be like if your team evolved from this—

Typical Hiring Results

—to this?

Topgrading Hiring

With almost all A Players, your team might need nine people, not twelve.

Chapter Summary

- Measure your costs of mis-hires.
- Measure your hiring success (percent A Players hired).
- Typical hiring results are 25 percent A Players (high performers), 50 percent Bs (good and fair), and 25 percent Cs (poor).
- Topgrading case studies show improvement from 26 percent to 85 percent high performers hired.
- Topgrading companies initially strive for 75% A Players hired, but after achieving it they raise the goal.

CHAPTER 4

Hiring Problem #1– Not Enough Applicants

Hiring talent remains the number one concern of CEOs in the most recent (2021, just before the pandemic) Conference Board Annual Survey; it's also the top concern of the entire executive suite. PwC's 2017 CEO survey reports that chief executives view the unavailability of talent and skills as the biggest threat to their business.

—Peter Cappelli, *Harvard Business Review*

Y ou need twenty-plus applicants (preferably more) to have a good chance of hiring an A Player.

If you have only half a handful of applicants, there is only a slim chance that tiny pool contains an A Player. Hiring the least bad candidate of a tiny pool of candidates pretty much assures disappointment. "But we *had* to hire somebody to head that region, or competitors would steal all of our business." Good point, so it's time to bite the bullet and do some things to *get more applicants*.

You know, all too well, pandemics can cause worker shortages. Aside from pandemics, clients over the years have struggled to find applicants because their industry is declining, the location is undesirable, their company culture is criticized by employees on social media, and on and on. The Great Resignation caused millions of job openings. Most new clients need to jack up recruiting in order to have a large enough applicant pool to hire an A Player. We have tracked how companies increase applicant pools and pass on the methods that work to our new and long-term clients.

A major retailer suffered from not enough applicants. You know the company, and it's super successful at attracting a lot of applicants easily—under normal circumstances. But they had miscalculated the difficulty of recruiting when the company was opening dozens of new stores in Florida and California at a time when unemployment was low. As one of the largest retailers in the US, they needed to hire thousands of associates, team leaders, and department managers. From the CEO down, the company was committed to hiring A Players in those jobs. The competencies were clear for the entry-level jobs: show the best customer service (treat everyone with respect and friendliness), be responsible and show up on time, work fast (but always take time to engage customers), stay on the job at least six months, and exhibit high integrity. Sounds like a solid plan, except …

At the time, unemployment was really low. Plus, the new stores were located within a couple miles of each other, competing with each other to hire the best people. At first, store managers just put Help Wanted signs in windows. Within a few months, district managers were becoming concerned—hiring standards were lowered because the stores *had* to fill jobs. The CEO didn't like that because unusually sharp stockers and cashiers helped define the company brand. Compounding the problem, turnover was unusually high. Snowbirds quit to head north in the summer. College students quit to return to school in the fall. Too many new employees were caught stealing, and customer complaints of unfriendly employees shot up. The CEO challenged the district managers, store managers, and HR to "Fix it!" They had to find ways to increase their applicant pools.

As mentioned, unemployment was low, applicant tracking systems had not been invented, and social media didn't exist. The new stores were not meeting targets because, desperate to hire, they settled for hiring the next warm body, and the mis-hires were destroying the company brand. We ran brainstorming meetings, and dozens of new ideas were considered.

Hiring Solution #1: Recruit the Right Way

Recruiting has become a way of life for us through Topgrading. Once we began to implement a Recruit from Networks policy, hiring has been quicker and more accurate. We have learned that A Players recommend other A Players at all levels in the company ... We find that this is a key to our hiring strategy.

—Frank Evans, CEO, Triton Management

What are the best, most effective ways to find qualified candidates for open positions?

The big-box retailer steadily implemented dozens of ways to recruit, and the new stores eventually succeeded. Among their recruiting methods: they paid employees referral fees for recommending friends, managers joined community organizations (asking members to recommend people), and the company held job fairs. They realized (finally!) that hiring high performers absolutely necessitates creating an applicant pool large enough to identify and hire A Players. Topgrading is understandably associated with executive hires, but the most successful case studies show the A Player standard being upheld all the way down to entry jobs, like cashiers (with much simpler hiring methods than for high-level jobs).

When you decide to recruit, a typical first step is to create a job description. Unfortunately, most job descriptions are vague, which contributes to mis-hires. Too often, a couple of months after a person has been hired, the new hire is thinking, "Holy cow—I had no idea I'd be held accountable for those high numbers" or "achieving results would require so much travel" or "my boss would have to approve every decision I make" or … The new hire's boss and others, all with somewhat different expectations, find their expectations are not very well met because they were not clearly defined or communicated to the new hire. Hiring against a vague job description causes confusion, unmet expectations, and (avoidable and expensive) mis-hires.

Recommended Exercise

Start your hiring process by creating a job scorecard.

Creating scorecards has made the biggest difference in hiring and keeping the best people because everyone now knows what A Player performance looks like. In the past, performance measurements were vague. Now we are all on the same page and we are getting A Player performance month in and month out.

—Travis Isaacson, Senior Director, Organization Development, Access Development

Most companies do not nail down performance accountabilities until after a person is hired. Why? It's a new role, and they want to be flexible—because they don't know what the market or competitors will do, they can't predict all the projects the new hire will be involved in, or they are just too busy dealing with daily crises. They may also erroneously believe that the new hire's goals will depend on what the new hire is good at—modifying the job to fit the person, rather than finding the right person for the role the business needs. They know they should have a performance management system with clear accountabilities and give team members regular performance feedback. A couple of months after hiring someone, they (finally) nail down what the new employee will be measured on so they know what to talk about in annual reviews, but they often don't take the time to clearly communicate those expectations to the new employee. Even worse, after (finally) defining those accountabilities, they may realize the new hire isn't a good fit and regret not taking the time to define specifics before they started recruiting. Chris and his team teach companies how to build job scorecards (with specific and measurable accountabilities) before recruiting candidates, to avoid all this confusion. And frankly, A Players demand to know what the job really is before they will accept an offer.

Consider a typical job description. For a key account manager, a list of requirements might include the following:

- Effective at capturing new accounts
- Excels at closing business deals
- Excellent communications
- Holds a college degree
- Three-plus years of relevant sales experience

A vague definition of *A Player* can lead to mis-hires. Job scorecards quantify accountabilities that define A Player performance, explain how the job is to be done (expected behaviors, core values, travel), and shape the nature of your recruitment to make it much more on target. Job scorecards describe exactly what an A Player looks like for a specific job.

Components of a Good Job Scorecard

- Requirements and technical skills (screening)
- Measurable accountabilities (what—results)
- Core values, key and important competencies (how—behaviors)

Steps to Create a Job Scorecard

1. List the *results* you expect a high performer to deliver, how they will be measured, and the target for each metric.
2. List your *core values*.
3. Identify *key competencies* (the behaviors in which an A Player must be *Excellent*).
4. List *requirements* (experience, education, certifications) and *technical skills*.

Job scorecards can be utilized for ...

- **Hiring.** You know exactly who you are looking for.
- **Onboarding.** You have expectations clearly defined before the person is hired so you can communicate those expectations on a new hire's first day.
- **Performance management.** You have the performance appraisal content created before a person is hired.
- **Measurement.** You can clearly determine whether a new hire is an A Player or not.

Need help finding recruitment software? Capteus is a free service, free because vendors pay a percent when they receive traffic.

Do this before recruiting and you'll recruit better candidates and hire better performers, and onboarding will be smoother. The probability that the new hire, manager, or coworkers will be surprised, shocked, disappointed, or frustrated is minimized. You will also have the clear basis for performance management. Finally, taking these steps will enable you to better measure the percent of high performers hired.

Recruitment Ideas to Consider

1. Write SEO-friendly job posts. Get some marketing help to properly structure and apply keywords to your posting. This is necessary for job hunters to find you.

2. Post the job on your website. Make sure it's a positive portrayal of the opportunity. Craft job ads that stand out, selling applicants on your company and the job. Get some marketing help to make your "Careers" or "Join Our Team" page exciting and reflective of your organization's culture. Check out companies you respect and your competitors for ideas to make this important but often overlooked part of your website stand out.

3. Encourage everyone to tap their network. The people who you, your managers, and your employees know usually include great candidates or people who can connect you to great candidates. "Birds of a feather flock together," and A Players on your team know A Players worth considering. Ann Drake built, and eventually sold, a successful logistics company. Every week in management meetings, she said, "Remember, team, we recruit all day, every day, with everyone we meet. That's how we avoid paying recruiters and we hire better people."

4. Pay referral fees to employees who recruit A Players from their personal networks. Most companies pay the bonuses as soon as the person is hired, not six months later "if" the person turns out to be an A Player. How much should you pay? It must be enough to incentivize people to stay in contact with A Players in their network.

5. In job ads, say whether the job is on-premises or virtual. A majority of applicants are pretty firm about which environment they prefer: virtual, in-office, or hybrid.

Topgrading, Inc. is a completely virtual organization, with employees spanning across the US, India, and South America. In late 2022, there are still many unknowns about what the best mix of virtual versus on-site might be for companies in various industries. At our (virtual) company, we favor hiring people who have already shown they can perform virtually. Specifically, they must have worked virtually and successfully for at least two years, and their boss has to have given them *Very Good* or *Excellent* performance ratings and confirm they are solid virtual employees.

6. Use job boards. Post your job ads where candidates can find them. This often requires paying a fee so that the sites' algorithms highlight your ad for job seekers they believe align with your posting. Having your ad appear on the first couple of pages of search results matters. If your company is in the SMB category, you may groan at this suggestion because of the costs associated with job boards. Big companies use them to augment their other sourcing tactics, and, yes, they can be expensive.

When you are desperate to hire and willing to look at a high volume of applicants (realizing that most will be unqualified), you may try using a job board. You've heard the ads. The best job boards have deep databases of professional and managerial contacts, and some will even push you résumés of active job seekers or "passive candidates" who may not be actively looking for another job.

Ultimately, you may get dozens or even hundreds of résumés, depending on how much you're willing to pay. But you may say, "The job boards get me mostly weak candidates. If I have a marketing opening for a seasoned pro and someone's résumé shows they have taken one marketing class years ago, the job board sends me that person's résumé." The job boards simply get you many more résumés; more résumés mean a higher probability of A Players being in that pool, and you have a better chance of hiring a high performer.

Be careful: "enabled recruiting applications" frequently don't work. These applications promise more and better candidates, but so far most have proven to be more hype than substance. Job hunters can Google how to game the system and fool you!

7. Increase compensation. Your pay must be competitive. When our clients say critical jobs have been open for a long time, a factor is often not increasing pay fast enough. Start with a place such as salary.com to see pay levels by function, level, and location to get a feel for the market. Search job boards to see what competitors are offering. (Some companies include compensation ranges in their job ads.) Consider engaging a compensation analyst to get even more precise.

8. Always be recruiting. Geoff Smart and Randy Street called this "building a virtual bench" in their book *Who.* Be on the lookout for A Players even when you don't have an open position to fill right now. If and when you do have an opening, a list of prescreened A Players you can call reduces the pressure to compromise and tends to result in that job getting filled quickly with an A Player.

Most of these recruitment methods can be initiated quickly. More time-consuming recruitment options are as follows:

9. Hire interns. Then you can "salt the mines" with talent and see them in action for an extended period of time.

10. Hire teachers and professors for summer or project work. Hire those who can recommend students you can hire for part-time, intern, or full-time jobs.

And for the most difficult option, consider doing what companies in high-tax/expensive-housing states do:

11. Consider relocating. This is the biggest step, for sure, and one that would likely be analyzed for at least a year. If candidates are few because your location is undesirable, consider relocating. Silicon Valley companies have been going to Texas and Arizona—not just for tax reasons but because workers cannot afford to live where they

HIRING PROBLEM #1—NOT ENOUGH APPLICANTS

worked, or they had to commute over an hour each way. Over the years, many of our clients have relocated to be able to attract more A Players. H-E-B, a multidecade client and now the #1 most respected grocery company in the US, moved their headquarters from Corpus Christi to San Antonio, Texas, in part to be able to recruit better candidates for executive positions.

Recommended Exercise

Measure more than your hiring success.

You've already been encouraged to measure your hiring success/ Quality of Hire and the cost of a bad hire because these exercises motivate teams to look for better hiring methods. You know that anything that's important must be measured in business, or it won't be done. Talent improves when related metrics are tracked. Initial measurements serve as a baseline so the team can set goals and gauge progress.

In addition to measuring Quality of Hire (percent of As hired) and costs of mis-hires (always more than people thought), our clients typically measure the following:

- **Percent of A Players on the team.** Improved hiring will increase this percentage. If not, maybe you're not retaining A Players because of a poor organizational culture, or you have too many B/C Player managers who drive away talent. The opposite could also be true—maybe you don't hire very well but quickly fire non-As, so the revolving door results in 80 percent high performers.
- **The number of applications you receive.** With twenty-plus per job, you'll be able to be selective, but thirty-plus betters your odds of hiring A Players.

- **The time it takes to fill jobs.** Faster is obviously better, but not at the expense of quality.
- **The quality of the candidate experience.** Ask candidates to rate it. You want people to feel good about the experience even if they do not receive a job offer. Revolving doors usually equal unhealthy organization culture, however.
- **Turnover/retention.** Improved hiring success will have limited positive impact if the A Players you hire don't stick around long enough. The Great Resignation was a wake-up call to treat employees better.

For all measurements, if the results are not good, the team digs in to find out both why this is the case and what the solutions are. If the funnel of applicants is not big enough, all the measurements typically disappoint. Effective hiring methods only work with lots of applicants, so it's necessary to recruit, recruit, recruit.

Chapter Summary

To progress with Topgrading beyond the "Topgrading first aid" level, achievable by using the solutions to five hiring problems, when you're ready please consider the following:

- Make your job ads and "Careers" page exciting, enticing, and engaging.
- Work to get twenty-plus applicants per opening, or you won't hire many A Players.
- Create a recruiting strategy that includes paying bonuses for employee referrals, leveraging team members' networks and paid postings on job boards.
- Define recruiting metrics, set targets, and hold the team accountable for achieving results.

CHAPTER 5

Hiring Problem #2— You Are Fooled into Hiring Low Performers

"Fool me once, shame on you. Fool me twice, shame on me."

Brad's Story

I almost quit my first full-time job as a professional interviewer of candidates for executive positions. Why? For several reasons, all of which relate to the big hiring problems you face. As a freshman in college, I knew I wanted a business career, but Business 101 was boring, and Psychology 101 was interesting. A local management psychologist taught a course in organizational psychology for one dollar, hoping to interest some students. I was interested!

I found several management psychology firms that interviewed and tested candidates for executive jobs, and one got me summer jobs in college and graduate school. So, I joined them after completing master's and PhD degrees—my first full-time job, Dr. Brad

Smart, Management Psychologist, expert interviewer. "Expert"? I had never conducted an interview and I had no idea if I'd be any good at it. And within a few weeks, I found that I didn't even enjoy interviewing. Clients mostly wanted us to somehow get candidates to not fool them, and I didn't want to try to trick candidates into admitting their failures and mistakes.

As the new kid on the block, I asked a question I should have asked years earlier:

Brad: "How good are we?"

Senior Partner: "What do you mean?"

Brad: "What percent of the candidates we assess and recommend and who are hired turn out to be high performers?"

Senior Partner: "I don't know—go introduce yourself to clients and ask them."

I did, and clients said our success rate was 33 percent. But their success in hiring high performers before using us was only 25 percent. And because executive mis-hires cost a fortune, clients figured that the ROI from using us was high enough. I considered it very low. I went home and told my wife, "Good grief! If I were a medical doctor and two-thirds of my patients left the hospital in body bags, I'd feel like a failure!"

It got worse. I quickly learned that verifying what candidates said in interviews was almost impossible because most companies discourage managers from taking reference calls for fear of a lawsuit by a former employee who said their former employer unfairly bad-mouthed them. Job seekers, confident that their prospec-

tive employer wouldn't try to talk with their managers, knew they could get away with hyping their successes and hiding mistakes. I wondered, "Could this reality help explain why you've been fooled by candidates?"

Talking with clients and my fellow professionals was discouraging. They agreed their low 25 percent and our 33 percent success rates (to me, ours was a 66 percent failure rate) were due to the "obvious" fact that people are not widgets and can't be evaluated like a new machine. Human beings are each unique, so "quality control" in hiring is impossible. People have normal defense mechanisms and tend to deny or ignore their shortcomings. So how can any interview elicit them? Or, when people do recognize their weaker points, they can easily hide them. And, people need jobs, so of course they'll put their best foot forward during the hiring process. It's just "human nature" to hype accomplishments and conceal mistakes. Conclusion: we're all supposed to shrug our shoulders and admit that consistently hiring high performers is a pretty much unattainable goal.

I soon added my own additional concerns about our profession.

We "experts" at hiring, with doctoral degrees, as outside inter-viewers, didn't fully understand the job the executive hire would have to do; we interviewed from their vague job description. Our sixty-minute interviews were the typical length for hiring but not nearly long enough to understand the candidate in any depth. The intelligence tests we administered in person seemed pretty accurate, but the accuracy of personality tests was hit and miss and, overall, did not accurately portray candidates. I'd taken many courses in testing at a doctoral level and knew that they *are useful when people are transparent and forthright (like when they are administered to existing employees for team building and leadership training) but poor for hiring, when people can easily give "right" responses. Over the years of our experience, when analyzing the effectiveness of using personality tests for screening, they can eliminate as many A Players as C Players. (Intelligence, ability, and knowledge tests are even suspect these days since candidates can take them off-site, perhaps getting a friend to take them or getting answers from the internet.)*

Half a century ago, and today, some candidates, surely low performers, were and are clever at not revealing their weaker points that would qualify them as mis-hires—or everyone wouldn't have so many bad hires. Our PhDs in psychology impressed clients, giving us an image of understanding humans at a deep level, but a PhD is a research degree requiring a scientific study and a dissertation. We understand statistics and experimental design, not necessarily how to "read" people. Psychologists on a path to counseling and therapy get a professional degree (PsyD); they are professionals who have better training to understand people's motivations, defense mechanisms, etc. At least my research degree produced one idea I had for a doctoral dissertation: to create a scientifically based hiring tool that would hopefully be a lot more effective than personality tests. And to complete this thought, hundreds of managers we've trained achieve even 90 percent high performers hired without that PhD. Way back then, my employer's clients didn't have a method of verifying what candidates said. They'd do background checks and call HR departments to get verification of job titles and years of employment, but the references they talked to all tended to be candidates' friends—not managers who really knew the candidates as employees.

Combined, all these concerns resulted in me mumbling to myself, during my first months employed, "Maybe I made a career mistake. Hiring isn't a 'profession'—it isn't even a function in companies that gets much respect because, obviously, hiring results suck." And in the many decades since, hiring methods continue to be poor for the same reasons that you, dear reader, recognize.

Maybe I was naïve, as well as stupid, but before abandoning my chosen "profession," I set out on a mission to find solutions.

The Big Underlying Problem: Transparency Is Almost Everywhere, but Not in Hiring

Consumer Reports helps you buy smarter. You can avoid buying a lemon by using CARFAX to see the full maintenance history. Search "Risks in …" and fill in the blank to see articles on the risks in buying thousands of products or services. For special-occasion dining, it's hard to beat Michelin or Zagat guides to get accurate restaurant ratings, and Yelp will show you the highest-rated pizza place in the area. Angi (formerly Angie's List) gives you ratings of service providers before you hire them. College students can avoid dull professors because student survey results are available that show real

> **Candidates can get accurate insights into your company, but you can't get accurate insights into your candidates. That is not fair.**

ratings and reviews. For people considering a job change and wondering if they would fit the organization culture, Glassdoor and Vault provide ratings and quotes from employees.

We're asked to rate products and services all the time. (How annoying is that!) But with hiring, how the heck do you get accurate ratings of candidate performance? Candidates can get accurate insights into your company, but you can't get accurate insights into your candidates. That is not fair.

Hiring managers and HR professionals experience mis-hires and often conclude, "When assessing candidates during the hiring process, we simply did not see the weaker points." You know why; the reality is that too many habitual low performers know they can exaggerate their strengths, hide their weaker points, and get away with it because most companies don't want their managers to take reference calls. On top of that, flawed hiring methods enable candidates to *easily* hide those weaker points throughout the hiring process, like in interviews and tests. Years ago, I (Brad) was shocked to learn these "truths."

How Serious Is the Problem of Applicants Lying to Get Jobs?

We consider it normal and smart for job seekers to put their best foot forward when job hunting. And we believe people are honest most of the time. Job seekers should research companies thoroughly to understand what they do, how they do it, the organization's culture, their core values, and what employees say about them. It's normal to search and get advice on how to write a résumé, how to answer interview questions, and what companies regard as acceptable and unacceptable responses. It's also normal for candidates to highlight their accomplishments and downplay mistakes. After all, we're all humans with defense mechanisms, and, for our own egos, we tend to see things through rose-colored glasses. Clients using Topgrading know that candidates research and learn what the hiring methods are, which is smart from the candidate's perspective. Our consistent message to job seekers over the years has been "Be open and honest, put your best foot forward, but don't try to game the system."

To claim untruthfully to have attended a certain college, attained a certain degree, or worked for some leading company crosses the line. For a candidate to change employment dates, hide companies they were fired from, or claim outstanding but false results also crosses the line. You don't want to hire someone who looks you in the eye and tells you they are someone who they are not or flat-out lies.

Statistics on Applicants Lying to Get Jobs

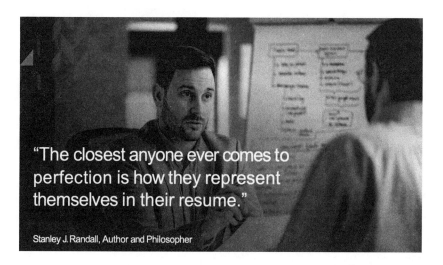

"The closest anyone ever comes to perfection is how they represent themselves in their resume."

Stanley J. Randall, Author and Philosopher

There are many published surveys (but not much solid science) regarding what percent of job seekers tells lies in their résumés and in interview responses. Here are some published statistics:

- BackgroundChecks.org: **57 percent** lied about skills; **55 percent** embellished responsibilities.
- Society for Human Resource Management: **86 percent** of four thousand HR members surveyed found lies.
- Stanford experiment: **92 percent** lied on both résumé and LinkedIn profile when offered a prize of $100 for creating the résumé best fitting a job they wanted.
- EmployeeScreenIQ: **50 percent** had discrepancies in job history.
- *Time* magazine: **43 percent** lied on résumés.
- HR conference in Hawaii: **90 percent** admitted to lying on résumés.
- HireRight: **27 percent** had serious lies in résumés.
- *Freakonomics*: cites literature showing **50 percent-plus** lied in résumés and interview responses.
- GradSchoolHub.com: **53 percent** of résumés and job applications contain falsifications.
- Topgrading, Inc.: three former background check professionals estimate that **40 percent** of applicants have at least one serious lie on their résumé.
- *Wall Street Journal*: **78 percent** of people admit that they would lie to get a job.

Considering these statistics and our career experiences, we can confidently say that more than half of applicants, consisting of a very high percentage of chronic low performers, cross the line. They exaggerate successes, say they did things that they did not actually do, and deliberately hide failures, mistakes, and weak points. The justifications are common: "Hiring is just a game … Everyone stretches the truth to get hired … I know I can do the job, despite not having performed or kept a job in the past ... What's the big deal? Everyone's social profiles are hype."

High performers, in both our experiences and our clients' experiences over decades, tend to be accurate and honest, not excessively hyping positives or hiding negatives. They *want you* to talk with their bosses, confident their bosses will sing their praises. High performers admit mistakes in interviews, in part because they can show a pattern of self-awareness and success in overcoming weaker points.

Is there a way to motivate all applicants to either be forthcoming or drop out?

Brad's Story (Continued)

A few months into my first job, I interviewed an executive who hired mostly high performers. I asked how, and the conversation went like this:

Manager: "Simple. I'm pretty successful at hiring because I get the best verification imaginable—I talk with the candidates' managers."

Brad: "Huh? How the heck can you do that when companies prohibit managers from taking reference calls?"

Manager: "Simple again. I tell the candidates up front that they eventually will have to ask their bosses to take a reference call. High performers are happy to try, and they almost always succeed in getting their bosses to talk."

Fascinated, I asked clients what they thought of this approach, and most said, "Let's try it." It worked. The Topgrading Truth Motivator was born. For years, we called it the TORC (Threat of Reference Check) technique, but A Players are eager to arrange the calls, knowing that their bosses will sing their praises. To them, it's a promise, not a threat. To C Players who have something to hide, it is a threat, but we changed the name anyway to the Topgrading Truth Motivator. Over the years, we've tweaked the method and found answers to common questions about how exactly to make the Truth Motivator work.

Hiring Solution #2: Use the Truth Motivator

Here it is: Let candidates know from the start that a final step in hiring is for them (not you) to arrange reference calls (usually when a job offer is on the table) with managers they've reported to and others with whom you'd like to talk. Clients loved it!

My work life immediately got 50 percent better because clients sent me transparent, forthcoming, and sharp candidates. Instead of trying to cleverly trick candidates into admitting their failures and shortcomings, when clients used the Truth Motivator, I got not only positives but negatives from honest high performers. A Players admit mistakes and are happy to explain how they fixed them and avoided similar mistakes in the future. Your work life will get better, too, for the same reason. Instead of trying to outsmart candidates to learn the whole truth, the Truth Motivator makes interviews an open, honest, two-way conversation. You learn more about candidates than you know about most of your friends, neighbors, and work associates. People are really inter-esting, and often fascinating, when they open up and tell you their *life and career story. With that knowledge, you can make the right hiring decisions.*

Naturally, just because candidates are forthcoming, it does not mean that they are necessarily the best fit for the job. Learning so much you can confidently rate managerial candidates on dozens of competencies will require you to become a student of interviewing for the remainder of your career. But that's fine; that's why we all try to master interviewing. Even after thousands of interviews, all our Topgrading professionals still learn something about interviewing techniques with every interview. But think of this: instead of starting interviews with a 50 percent chance you'll be faced with hype and concealment, you can look forward to finding most of the people you interview very open and transparent, not hyping accomplishments, and amazingly willing to admit mistakes and failures. They'll trust you to be fair in judging the "real" them.

Back in my first year as a professional, clients who didn't use the Truth Motivator sent me candidates that played the game of hyping and concealing, and so interviewing candidates for them was, you know, frustrating. Fortunately, for the past few decades, all our clients have used the Truth Motivator, so we have not had to cope with the game-playing frustrations. We hope and fully expect that you will be thrilled with your in-depth interviews and hiring results because of a refreshingly high level of candidate candor and transparency.

Recommended Exercise

Get far better candidates from recruiters by requiring them to explain the Truth Motivator.

Retained search firms get paid (up to a third of first-year compensation) regardless of whether you hire someone or not. Almost all large and medium-sized firms use retained search firms for top executive jobs because those firms typically have zillions of executive contacts. For each of the last three editions of *Topgrading*, two hundred CEOs were asked "What percent of the time, when you've used an executive search firm, have you been satisfied with the result?" The average: 20 percent—meaning that 80 percent of the time CEOs said they did *not* get their money's worth using executive search firms.

Why so low? Too often, search consultants produce sugarcoated reports that do not include any of candidates' significant weaker points. They don't ask for negatives, don't get them, and don't put them in reports to their clients. You and we know that everyone, including A Player candidates, have made mistakes (and learned from them), and all of us have some areas for improvement (even you and us).

Fortunately, there are a couple of things you can do that will get you better candidates. Require search consultants to (a) ask candidates in their interviews not just for successes in every job but for mistakes and boss ratings, (b) put all that information in their reports, and (c) only present candidates who have been told about and are willing to arrange calls with managers. Search firms doing this get high ratings from clients.

Clients don't want us recommending their search executives, for fear that they will become too busy to serve them, but we know of boutique firms that use Topgrading. Yes, they create detailed Job Scorecards, use the Topgrading Truth Motivator, and they use recruitment tools such as LinkedIn Recruiter to wash out most candidates and present clients with mostly A Players.

Contingency recruiters are typically used for lower-level roles and are only paid if you hire someone they present. They usually send résumés but no report. *Ask all contingency recruiters and your internal recruiters to tell the candidates they present to you that a final step in hiring is for them, the candidates, to arrange reference calls with bosses, at a time when they are comfortable doing so.* With this simple action, you will definitely get better candidates from recruiters and know that you're interviewing basically honest high performers. They may not necessarily be a good fit for the job, but other hiring steps will determine that.

You just learned this "Recommended Exercise" in the minute you took to read it. Follow that advice, and it will save you a lot of time and money, because all three categories of recruiters (search, contingency, and internal) have historically presented too many mediocre or poor candidates. Take this advice, and overnight they will begin presenting much, much better candidates.

When Larry Bossidy was CEO of Honeywell, he cut forty executive search firms to four and made it very clear: to be one of the four firms, their search consultants had to use Topgrading methods. We got calls from the largest firms, and most were willing to send their people to our public workshops, but that wasn't necessary. Our simple message to executive search consultants is: Continue using chronological career interviews but only present candidates to clients if they have been told the Truth Motivator, and only if their reports show successes, failures, strengths, and weaker points in each job.

It worked for Honeywell. For example, the aerospace plant in Phoenix improved hiring when a major executive search firm had placed one of their consultants full-time in the plant. The plant measured several hiring stats, and hiring success improved. Their on-site recruiter only presented candidates who in fact did arrange reference calls with their managers. The hiring manager and HR conducted those reference calls. You can send the above three requirements to the recruiters you hire.

The Benefits of Using the Topgrading Truth Motivator

It works. Almost everyone you interview will be more forthcoming and transparent. Evidence about the efficacy of the Truth Motivator will be strong the very first time you try it. Ask candidates in the Topgrading interview (chapter 5) how bosses would rate them, and when you talk with those bosses in reference calls (chapter 6), you'll experience how powerful the Truth Motivator is. Why? Candidates accurately guess how managers will rate their performance and what managers will say about their strengths and weaker points!

Low performers who "crossed the line" in their résumé drop out. Ideally, they upload their résumé and/or filled out an application and then learned about the Truth Motivator. They realize they will not get their bosses to talk with you, and they wouldn't *want* them to talk with you since you would probably hear negative opinions. You still have their résumé and can call them, but the applicants with fictitious résumés are essentially "busted." You save money.

Your screening is reduced about 50 percent, not having to waste time reading résumés or phone reviewing habitual low performers. This saves you money and makes hiring faster.

Greater candidate transparency makes any interview you conduct better, and it strengthens your coaching. You will instantly realize your interviewees are more forthcoming, making your interviews more revealing and, frankly, more fun for you to conduct. Our clients and Topgrading professionals learn many more details about candidates' strengths and also their weaker points, the ones hiring managers need to know about to be sure they make the right hiring decision. Sometimes candidates reveal weaker points that can be overcome or controlled, so you can be confident that the person can perform as an A Player. Coaching can begin at once, since you know their strengths that can be maximized and their weaker points that they need to overcome.

The Truth Motivator is almost a panacea. For hundreds of thousands of managers, it has been career-changing and even life-changing. The Truth Motivator is the first step toward finally building teams of almost all A Players. These managers perform better, which converts to faster promotions for them and their team members. And more successful careers can lead to more happiness and fulfillment in life.

Is Topgrading fair and ethical? Let's pause for a moment and look at the big picture. Is motivating people to disclose their weaker points the

> Your screening is reduced about 50 percent, not having to waste time reading résumés or phone reviewing habitual low performers.

right and fair thing to do? We believe so, because the "state of hiring" is shady, with too many people fudging the truth to get jobs. With a lot more openness and honesty, everyone would win.

It's not a great commentary on human nature but ... in most countries, it is socially acceptable to (wink) cheat a little to get a job. We encourage job seekers, for starters, to look for jobs where they can be a high performer and not ones where they will be paid more but fall short of expectations. And then we recommend that candidates be forthcoming and not hype positives or hide key weaker areas.

Unfortunately, too many low performers try to fake their way into higher paying jobs, where they don't perform well, rather than being forthcoming and seeking lower-paying jobs where they could shine, perhaps eventually qualifying for promotions. That's their problem, so don't feel guilty for setting and maintaining high standards and for rejecting candidates who were not forthcoming with you.

At the end of this book, we offer a challenge to businesses to encourage managers to take reference calls, even when their honest appraisal of a former employee is negative.

Chapter Summary

- The single biggest problem in hiring, in one sentence: Candidates can fool you because they assume they can get away with it when companies discourage managers from taking reference calls.
- More than 50 percent of applicants lie on their résumé and continue the fiction in interviews, tests, and reference checks with buddies.
- Use the Topgrading Truth Motivator to motivate candidates to either be forthcoming or drop out—so screening time is reduced by 50 percent. You save time, so you save money.
- Get much better performance from recruiters by requiring them to only present candidates who agree to arrange reference calls with their managers (at the appropriate time, usually when they have a job offer).
- The Truth Motivator makes hiring, onboarding, and coaching more effective.
- Topgrading is fair and ethical.

CHAPTER 6

Hiring Problem #3– Shallow, Unrevealing Interviews

The Tandem Topgrading Interview, using the Topgrading Interview Guide, has become critical to our staffing process. It is set up in a logical and systematic way. It allows the interviewers to hear a thorough review of candidates' education and all full-time jobs— how they got to where they are today—the events, motivations, accomplishments, and failures. It's really opened our eyes to important things that we otherwise would have missed and, more than anything else, accounts for our hiring more A Players.

—Rick Steinberg, VP Human Resources, Columbus McKinnon

Brad's Story (Continued)

As mentioned in the last chapter, I wasn't happy in my first job, interviewing candidates for executive positions. One reason was that clients expected us, as professional interviewers, to learn what they couldn't—when candidates are truthful, or not, particularly when describing their successes and mistakes. But, though we were all PhD psychologists, we honestly couldn't be sure either.

My doctoral studies emphasized the long histories of interviewing and testing. But while dozens of components of psychological theory go into interviewing and should have made interviewing highly valid, they didn't.

In my first week on the job, I sat in on an interview with the senior partner, who conducted an interview for a second-level marketing candidate for a big insurance company. My expectations were high. I had taken plenty of doctoral-level courses on interviewing and testing. Then, and now, there was evidence that the best interviews were structured (all candidates were asked the same questions), and so the questions all related to the skills needed to perform the job. Although the hundreds of studies I'd read failed to show respectable validity of hiring interviews and totally ignored how to hire high performers, I figured these professionals out in the real world must have some special techniques to boost hiring success.

The client had sent over a job description, but it was vague, nothing like a job scorecard. There was no standard interview guide. The interview was sixty minutes long and consisted of seemingly random questions based on the candidate's résumé, plus a few competency questions relevant to the job. Prior to the interview, a battery of tests was administered, including two cognitive tests, two personality tests, and Rorschach inkblots. I had hoped to learn how to interpret the test results—grad school didn't teach that—but, although my coworkers offered opinions, they were confusing. At the end of the interview, I was lost. I'd read a bunch of candidate reports, but they seemed to waffle—the candidate is sometimes organized, sometimes not, sometimes an effective decision maker, sometimes not, sometimes good with people ... You get the point.

I was far from being confident about any of the candidate's strengths or weaknesses. I was left with nothing more than some weak hunches—far from "nailing" whether the candidate would be an A, B, or C Player. We professionals never conducted reference checks—clients would ask candidates to give them names of references they called, but clients said that naturally they were only given permission to call people on the list who only said positive things about the candidates. Clients also called HR departments but just to get confirmation of dates of employment and job titles. So, reference calls and HR information would not give me useful information. But I had one more chance to gain insights.

At the end of the senior partner's interview he asked, "Brad, do you have any further questions?"

I said yes, but it was time for lunch, so I asked if the candidate would come back after lunch. He agreed, but I skipped lunch—as a brand-new interviewing "expert," I had to figure out what questions I'd ask. The short, shallow, unrevealing interview I'd observed was so scattered I had to try a different approach. Hmm ... there were clinical psychological "intake interviews" that covered a person's history, but these focused too much on early home influences and not much on the person's career. So, I decided to conduct a business-oriented chronological interview covering all jobs, asking questions for each job about mistakes, weaker points, and performance ratings by managers. This was the first crack at what became the Topgrading interview.

Meekly I said to the candidate, "We met this morning. You know I'm new, and, honestly, you are my first interviewee. Would it be okay if I conduct a full-career interview?" He agreed. Phew!

Luckily, the candidate was an A Player, very willing to participate in this walk down memory lane, and loved bragging about his accomplishments. But he also admitted mistakes and failures—maybe because he explained how he overcame them, or maybe because he had many more accomplishments to talk about than mistakes that were made. I hadn't discovered the Truth Motivator yet, but of course A Players can brag without hyping their responses.

After the interview, I felt relieved when he said, "Dr. Smart, I think you know a lot more about me than Dr. X [the senior partner] who interviewed me this morning."

I spent the next morning writing a report and asked the senior partner if he wanted to read it. He said something like, "No, send it to the client, CEO, and HR; this is a test since that was your first solo interview." Gulp.

I sent the report, and two days later he called me into his office, clearly not happy. Uh-oh. He said, "I have your report here, twelve pages long, next to mine, which is only two pages. I'll be frank with you, Brad." Uh-oh, my report must have sucked! "When the client said they loved your report, I read it—and mine is crap compared to yours." Verbatim.

Good news, right? Yes and no. The senior partner said my salary required me to conduct four interviews and write four reports daily. I said I was brand-new on the job and not ready to assess four candidates daily. That was a delaying tactic—I had no intention of abandoning the more revealing interview method I'd tried.

I continued to conduct four-hour interviews with executive candidates. I got pressure from the whole firm to adopt their hiring methods, and I refused, nicely, for one simple reason: clients soon reported that they were sure that a higher percentage of my recommended candidates would succeed. I offered this suggestion: "How about the rest of you conduct more thorough chronological interviews and write more informative reports, which will result in our clients hiring more A Players?" No sale. "And I'm very sure that if they know that their mis-hires are declining they'll be willing to pay us more." No sale. "But," I said, "our clients estimate the costs of mis-hires at the C-suite level to be millions of dollars. We could charge ten times our fees, and they wouldn't blink if we documented the reduced cost of mis-hires." No response.

You can guess the rest of the story. No one agreed to change their interview method, so I left and eventually started Topgrading, Inc.

The Topgrading interview—chronological, in-depth, and structured—is the most powerful, difficult, thorough, revealing interview you will ever conduct. The depth of insight you'll get is powered by a combination of the Truth Motivator and thoroughness—a full-career interview. With practice, you can learn to do it well.

When you were first promoted to a leadership position, you probably weren't trained to interview people. Most leaders must figure out interviewing on their own. We've noticed an odd paradox over the years. In public, most leaders say, "I'm a pretty good interviewer; I have good instincts about people." But in meetings in which they rate their team's performance, they are frustrated when they reveal that they suffered from many "so-so" performers, mis-hires.

Your hiring approach probably has tied both your hands behind your back, metaphorically. You can likely become a very good interviewer over time, but your current approach does not motivate candidates to be totally honest (one hand tied). And even if you use a structured competency-interview approach, you conduct hopelessly shallow interviews that cannot possibly clue you into the whole truth about all the competencies necessary to avoid almost all mis-hires (the second hand tied). You know this to be true because when the hiring team rates candidates on the (too few) key competencies and then hires people, they commonly look back at the hiring process and ask, "What went wrong? Our ratings were way off." We're out of hands to tie, but a third problem is that you're not given enough time for a full-career interview. You simply can't get to know someone very well in an hour.

You Aren't Failing—Your Hiring Method (Especially Your Interview Method) Is Failing You

In addition to using your usual screening tools—phone screen interviews and any other interviews in your process—adding the Topgrading interview is what will suddenly, for the first time in your career, reveal deep insights into not just a few but *all* the competencies necessary for someone to perform at the A Player level.

Too many companies are stuck with a hiring policy that imposes mediocre interview methods on managers (which is what Brad faced in his first job). We feel strongly that if hiring were medicine, the lack of a good, comprehensive, chronological interview is like a hospital not having a policy for doctors scrubbing their hands before surgery. Atul Gawande shook up the medical world with his best-selling book *The Checklist Manifesto*. The book showed how hospitals caused one hundred thousand more deaths per year because thorough procedures and policies were *not* followed. Hospital policies rarely assure that *all* checklist activities will be done. Scary, huh? In his introduction, Gawande cited an extremely thorough hiring method that, when followed consciously, produced better hiring; that method is—Topgrading.

Decades ago, typical interviews were haphazard, with vague questions like "Tell me about yourself," hypothetical questions like "How would you handle a leadership challenge such as employees threatening to unionize?" and questions with no validity such as "What's your favorite color and why?" As you know, artificial intelligence and bots are becoming more prevalent as hiring tools—with mostly poor results plus legal and ethical issues. Ability and knowledge tests can add value, unless a candidate's friend takes them or answers are found online. Personality tests are easily gamed. (Search "how to ace the [fill in the name of the test].") It's easy for candidates to find information about how to pass tests; that's why personality tests can eliminate as many A Players as C Players. We'll

Today's hiring approaches are a "dog's breakfast" of methods that don't work.

discuss these issues and suggest what you should do, and not do, a little later.

Today's hiring approaches are a "dog's breakfast" of methods that don't work. Because interviews are the most important tool for assessing candidates, let's dig in a bit more to the most common interview approach: competency/behavioral interviews.

Competency/Behavioral Interviews

They are called *competency/behavioral interviews* because the questions are directed at the behaviors or competencies identified for the particular job. They are "behavioral" because most ask for actual behaviors. Instead of "How organized are you?" a question might be "Will you please describe a time when you were well organized and a time when you were not so well organized?" For brevity, we'll refer to them just as *competency interviews*. When Topgrading replaces another hiring method, it's usually a method based on competency interviews with a success rate of 25 percent high performers hired.

The doctoral dissertation referred to earlier (by Dr. Michael Lorence, Georgia State University) reported that after a year of experience using Topgrading methods, additional competency interviews were abandoned by one-third of the organizations studied. That said, the fact is that most large organizations use competency interviewing. Several companies sell their version of a "plug-and-play" hiring method created in the 1960s and have not improved much since, except that now they integrate with human resources systems (HRS).

The competency-interview method, which in the 1960s was a huge step forward in professionalism, involves something like this:

- Pick six or eight key competencies for the job.
- Use the library of behavioral interview questions for those competencies.
- Be sure all candidates are asked the same questions (which is good because the Equal Employment Opportunity Commission loves structure that minimizes bias and prejudice).
- Each interviewer creates their own follow-up questions, generated on the spot and triggered by answers to standard questions.
- Meet with other interviewers at the end of the day to compare notes, so the committee agrees on the ratings of the candidate on all key competencies.

Why are the hiring results of competency interviews not so hot?

1. **They address too few competencies.** As we've stated, literally dozens of competencies should be addressed for a managerial job. Why? It's almost impossible for a manager, for example, to be rated *Poor* on any competency and still qualify as an A Player. If many critical competencies aren't even considered, you are shooting in the dark, guessing if someone is a good candidate with very limited, partial information. It's like a pilot's checklist if 90 percent of the checks are not made. Or, competency interviews are like Swiss cheese—lots and lots of holes. You will soon learn that Topgrading Interviews are like cheddar cheese—no holes.

2. **They have too few questions about each competency.** It's common to have eight competencies, with four interviewers each responsible for questions about two competencies in a half-hour interview. In that half hour, maybe six questions can be asked and answered, with follow-up questions and

answers. It's impossible to get insight into how strong each competency is with a "snapshot."

3. **They lack integration.** With "snapshots" rather than a biographical "movie" of the candidate, it's impossible to comprehend how each competency interacts and overlaps with all the other competencies. This relates to the parable of the blindfolded people and the elephant. For example, the rating on *Organizational Skills* might be high, contradicting the low rating on *Planning* (which requires good organizational skills). There is no way the method resolves how ratings based on competencies can contradict each other. No patterns = no integration = no clarity.

4. **They reveal too little of what you need to know.** At the end of the competency-interview day, the interviewers meet to gain consensus on how to rate the (eight) competencies and whether to continue with the candidate or not. But consensus is missing, and, theoretically, even if all (eight) ratings are high, the interviewers sometimes want to reject the candidate—because they gave negative insights into other important competencies that were not included in the process.

5. **They are easy to "ace."** By now you know that just about everything in competency interviews can be exaggerated or flat-out faked. And too often they *are* faked, since candidates are sure that their managers won't be called upon to rate them. There are books on how to get a job that encourages hyping and hiding. Some outplacement counselors help people write hyped résumés and role-play how job seekers can spin answers. In our society, it is socially acceptable to fudge the truth to get a job.

To be fair to competency interviews, if you add the Truth Motivator to your process, at least candidates will be more honest, as they answer the inadequate "snapshot" questions. But getting honest answers when too few questions are asked about too few competencies results in confusion and explains why many organizations skip competency interviews altogether.

How the Tandem Topgrading Interview Was Perfected at the World's Most Valuable Company

No company can expect to beat the competition unless it has the best human capital. Topgrading is the definitive method to gain that advantage.

—Larry Bossidy, Chairman and CEO, Honeywell (retired) and Executive Chairman, General Electric, during the Topgrading years

With Topgrading, we hired and promoted three times more people who turned out to be A Players.

—Jack Welch, CEO, General Electric (retired in 2001)

Before teaching you a light version of this interview, there is one more story that will be our last word on competency interviewing. The General Electric story is two decades old, but they used Topgrading methods to become the most valuable company in the world at the time. The Tandem Topgrading interview method was perfected at GE.

Brad's Story (Continued)

In the 1980s, CEO Jack Welch was very frustrated with the company's 25 percent success rate when it came to hiring and promoting. He wanted A Players in every job. So, in 1988 he sent out one hundred human resources executives to find the best hiring method. The CHROs found me, as well as the top competency-hiring expert at that time. We're sharing this story since today many companies have not heard of Topgrading and use competency interviewing—with mediocre results.

A "shoot-out" was staged in which Mr. Competency Interviewer interviewed someone behind a one-way window with one hundred observers, the GE chief human resource officers (CHROs). He had previously identified eight competencies appropriate for his competency interview with a senior manager candidate. I did not observe. In the afternoon, I interviewed the same executive using the Topgrading interview. Topgrading was chosen—one hundred to zero in votes. Why? The CHRO evaluations were very consistent: the competency interview only focused on eight competencies; the Topgrading interview focused on dozens. The competency interview lasted only ninety minutes and consisted of ten standard questions (plus follow-ups) for each competency. The Topgrading interview lasted four hours and was a chronological interview covering education years, ten standard questions plus follow-up questions for all fifteen jobs, and questions about future goals. The competency interview "in real life" would have been supplemented with reference checks done by the people the candidate recommended, plus confirmation of candidate job titles and dates from the HR departments of previous employers. The Topgrading interview started with statement of the Truth Motivator. The *interviewee agreed to it, and further verification would also have been with a background check and information from HR departments of previous employers. But, more importantly, the candidate would have arranged reference calls with managers he reported to. In short, the problems with competency interviews described at the beginning of this chapter were confirmed by one hundred top human resources executives of the time.*

Thousands of GE managers were trained as Topgrading was rolled out. Managers participated in two-day workshops, covering all the components of the methodology, with a full day devoted to the Topgrading interview. By 1995, GE was achieving 50 percent A Players hired and promoted—doubling their success and seeing the company sales and profits soaring. Were we satisfied? Nope. Were Larry and Jack (always referred to by their first names) satisfied? Nope. So, we sat in on workshops and saw these very sharp HR executives ... struggling. Let's face it—interviewing is difficult. These executives were trained but had other responsibilities in addition to interviewing candidates.

So, we inserted a second interviewer—the first Tandem Topgrading Interviews. And bam! Instantly the interviews were more revealing and a heck of a lot easier for both interviewers. And that's when GE hired almost 90 percent A Players, and their revenues shot up to #1 in the world.

Think of it this way. Would you want to hire managers by judging them on résumés with questionable accuracy, only eight competencies studied, short interviews that elicit their idealized Facebook or LinkedIn profile, and weak verification? Or would you prefer to hire managerial candidates with accurate résumés and

*focus on all the important competencies, much more thorough
interviews, and honest responses elicited, and with the best verification imaginable—reference calls with managers?*

Hiring Solution #3:
Conduct Topgrading Interviews

*Hill-Rom Human Resources leaders and hiring managers are
totally reliant on the Topgrading Interview Guide to drive accurate
interview conclusions. It ensures the interviewer will stay on point,
ask consistent questions, and gain a comprehensive understanding
of the applicant's work behaviors. Hill-Rom leaders, at the end of
their interview, are 90 percent confident they know the employment
candidate's work behavior tendencies. The outcomes are a 90
percent-plus successful hire and retention rate.*

—John Dickey, SVP Human Resources, Hill-Rom

You've already learned a fair amount about Topgrading Interviews,
and you understand the value of using an interview partner, so you're
ready for your basic course in *how*. We start with how difficult interviewing is. When you conduct interviews, you have many things you
must do correctly:

- Ask the standard questions.
- Listen carefully to answers.
- Compare those answers with other answers to see how they
  blend or conflict.
- Create original follow-up questions on the spot.
- Take comprehensive notes.

- Try to make sense of body language.
- Wonder if it's time for a break.
- Avoid asking "leading questions."
- Try to control bias or prejudice.
- Remember not to frown (a risk if you're concentrating hard).
- Introduce a little humor to keep rapport high.
- Use the candidate's name at least every fifteen minutes to not appear cold.
- Keep enough but not too much eye contact for rapport. (Your mom was right. "Don't stare.")
- Maintain control; don't let the interviewee go off on tangents or avoid your questions.
- Look for patterns of strengths and weaker points as you move through jobs.
- Remember the many different patterns to be able to ask good follow-up questions.
- Watch for "red flags," like a sudden loss of eye contact or change in voice volume (indicators that the interviewee might be hiding something).
- Avoid jumping to conclusions.
- Toward the end of the interview, test your hunches. ("You've said your managers have tended to load you up with too many projects. I'm guessing you are very hesitant to push back, even when working far more than forty hours?")

Because of interview complexity, you can understand why the tandem interview is so popular. Both interviewers can take mental breaks and be confident that their partner can come in, ask questions, etc. If you don't connect some dots, there is a good chance your partner will. There is a primary interviewer, who asks *most* questions and takes *some* notes, and a secondary interviewer, who asks *some* questions and takes *lots* of notes. They can switch roles from time to time to get mental breaks. Together they see the patterns of how each competency evolved from job to job, and by the time they finish the interview, they are pretty sure of their ratings. After the interview, the interviewers review their notes and arrive at a consensus on how to rate the candidate on all competencies and whether the candidate is good enough to ask them to arrange reference calls. That dialogue helps both interviewers clarify their opinions, so they are very sure of their joint ratings and hire/no-hire conclusions.

These days, almost all Topgrading Interviews are conducted by two interviewers. An exception is for lower-level jobs, where the hiring methods are shorter and simpler. When the jobs are entry level, such as grocery stocker, a service operations manager conducts a solo Topgrading interview in about thirty minutes, just focusing on the most recent five years. Another exception is when Topgrading interviewers are used for executive hires. Chris and his Topgrading professionals are capable of doing solo interviews but welcome hiring managers (even the CEO) to participate in interviews. Hiring managers learn from watching someone who has conducted thousands of interviews. They can ask great follow-up questions and see how professionals probe so deftly that their conclusions are rock solid.

Pick an Interview Partner

Make yourself, the hiring manager, one of the interviewers. If someone in human resources is a terrific interviewer, great. Ask them to be your partner. Oftentimes they become the best interviewers because they get to conduct many interviews. If you don't have an HR function, ask another respected member of the team to be your partner, maybe an expert in the function that you're hiring for. If you're a general manager and hiring your first director of marketing, pick a marketing expert, an associate or consultant, to be your partner.

To reduce bias, try to pick an interview partner who is the same gender, race, age, etc., as the interviewee. For diversity, you might add a third interviewer, but three is maximum. Don't make it a "pile on"; the three of you agree in advance that the primary interviewer will ask about 90 percent of the questions, and the other two try to ask no more than 5 percent each.

How to Conduct a Topgrading Interview (of a Manager)

PREPARATION

Study the candidate's job scorecard, résumé, and LinkedIn profile, and if you used the PreScreen Snapshot for Screening (chapter 7), review that quickly. Let managerial candidates know that this is a three- to four-hour interview.

DURING THE INTERVIEW

Greeting. Be friendly, explain the chronology, and repeat the Truth Motivator (asking if they agree to arrange reference calls at the appropriate time).

Education years. For high school, college/university, and any further education years, ask the following:

- "What were some high and low points?"
- "Through your teen years, who were major influencers (coaches, parents, or others)? And how did they influence

who you are today in terms of your career goals, personality, and values?"

Chronological job history. For every full-time job, starting with the first, ask the following:

- "Why did you take that job?"
- "What were your key responsibilities?"
- "What were your major successes and accomplishments?"
- "What mistakes did you make?"
- "What did you like and dislike about the job?"
- For leaders: "Tell me about the team you inherited. What percent were A Players (*Excellent* or *Very Good* performers you'd enthusiastically rehire); B Players (*Good*, solid performers); and C Players (*Fair* or *Poor* performers)?"
- "What percentage of A, B, and C Players did you end up with?"
- "What actions did you take with your team—training, coaching, hiring, firing?"
- "What was your manager's name? What did you like and dislike about your boss?" (Look for patterns. Do you as hiring manager fit the pattern the candidate likes?)
- "Keep in mind a final step in hiring will be for you to arrange calls with bosses and a couple of peers and direct reports. What's your best guess as to how [boss's name] would rate your performance? And what would they list as your strengths and weaker points?" (The patterns here give you the most valuable insights into candidates.)
- "Why did you leave that job?"

Plans for the future. "What are your short- and long-term future plans, along with your career goals?"

Job applied for. "From what you know about the job and company, what do you like most and least about the opportunity?"

END THE INTERVIEW

Tell the candidate you'll review your notes and get back to them within a day. If the candidate is interested and you are too, say, "We'll get back to you, and assuming we, too, are enthusiastic, we'll ask you to arrange some reference calls."

WRITE A BRIEF CANDIDATE SUMMARY AFTER THE TANDEM TOPGRADING INTERVIEW

Compare notes. Both interviewers should take half an hour to review their own notes. Then get together and rate the candidate on all competencies; share notes and thoughts, argue, and then make your joint rating. After doing this for all competencies, decide on your tentative conclusion—hire or not hire. This is sort of like a jury deliberating. Relate all your data to the job scorecard.

If the tentative decision is positive, ask the candidate to arrange reference calls (chapter 7). Then one of you write a summary—your combined final conclusion (hire or not hire), listing key strengths and weaker points.

Congratulate one another. You gained a deeper understanding of all competencies, more than ever before. And you don't just "hope" the person will perform as an A Player; after your thorough interview and consistently positive comments from managers in reference calls, you're sure of it.

Culture Fit and the Topgrading Interview

New clients commonly say that measuring cultural fit is pretty easy after a Topgrading interview. Why? Almost every question in the interview relates to culture fit. "Why did you take the job?" always relates to culture. Ditto for what they liked and disliked about the job, and why they left. Accomplishments and failures occur within the company culture and impact results. All the questions about their managers relate to culture, and when you actually do the reference calls with those bosses, just about everything they tell you will relate to how well your candidate fit their culture.

If the founder/owner/CEO/board is determined to change the culture, to drive new strategic directions, to change the work locations, to go international, or to open the culture to more diversity—a candidate who beautifully fit the existing culture, the old way of doing things, might be a terrible fit for what is now desired.

> A candidate who beautifully fit the existing culture, the old way of doing things, might be a terrible fit for what is now desired.

Culture fit and transparency are two-way streets. The Truth Motivator asks candidates to be honest, so you should be honest with candidates about chinks in your (cultural) armor. When you ask "From what you know about the job and company, what do you like most and least about the opportunity here?" be prepared to hear and respond to legitimate questions about the company, the job, and your leadership style. A

Players want (actually, require) to analyze you and the company, sort of reference checking both, by asking their questions during interviews.

Chris has watched tens of thousands of managers conduct their first Tandem Topgrading interview, and though they slipped a little at various times, they pushed on through to completion, knowing that they learned, by far, the most important information about the candidate and were determined to always use this type of interview and improve with practice.

Topgrading Interviews Overcome the Problems of Competency Interviews (Too Few Questions, Too Short, Lacking Integration, Confusing/ Contradictory Conclusions, Easy to Fake)

Thoughtfully review the sequence (above) of Topgrading interview questions. You can now sense how you will, with the questions and answers about every job, gather accurate insights into dozens of competencies and, with each job, learn how the candidate grew within many of the competencies. For example, an explanation of a significant accomplishment like winning the President's Award for getting a critical, complex project done on time and under budget will reveal at least two dozen competencies spread across multiple categories: intellectual, personal, interpersonal, leadership, and motivational. Insights revealing competencies occur as candidates share details of many, many accomplishments and successes and examples of mistakes made and lessons learned. The result, of course, is very accurate conclusions about ratings on all competencies and confidence that you will make good decisions, whether it be to hire or not hire.

Topgrading Interviews Save a Ton of Time!

Topgrading Interviews are typically three hours long for a mid-manager (times two interviewers) plus another hour sharing notes and arriving at conclusions. That's eight hours of total interview time. A common argument we hear is "We're so busy. How can we take eight hours for one interview?" Topgrading Interviews are only conducted with finalist candidates, and the Topgrading Truth Motivator and PreScreen Snapshot (chapter 8) help you accurately and efficiently cull the applicant pool so that you are spending time with fewer but higher-quality candidates. Out of the starting gate, Topgrading saves you time. And after learning about competency-interview problems, you can see how they can be reduced or skipped altogether, saving more time. Our clients report that when they use all the solutions in this book simultaneously, it can cut total time invested to fill an open position by half or more.

Consider this. Our research shows that mis-hired, low-performing mid-managers cost their manager and coworkers two hundred hours preventing and fixing the problems they caused. At the risk of oversimplifying, hiring a high performer and avoiding a mis-hire might require interviewing three finalists for six hours (two interviewers for three hours each). That's eighteen hours total (six hours × three candidates). Wow! Eighteen hours spent on just one opening? Yes, but that means 182 hours *not wasted* preventing and fixing problems caused by a mis-hire (200 − 18 = 182).

Virtual Interviews Using a Webcam Are "Real Enough" to Assess Candidates, Even for Top Jobs

It was easy during the pandemic to go completely virtual for hiring lower-level jobs. Candidates and interviewers liked the convenience. In the first weeks of the pandemic, there was a crisis mentality. "OMG, we *can't* hire executives with a phone call or choppy video call because no one can really connect or read body language or be real." With in-person interviews impossible, due to various forms of lockdowns, of course companies tried virtual interviews, and—surprise, surprise—there were almost no problems. Current technology is of higher quality than earlier options. Scheduling is easier. Rescheduling is simple. And the time and expense of travel are eliminated. What's most important: the percent of high performers hired is still extremely high with virtual Tandem Topgrading Interviews. And yes, for executive hires, *after* the virtual Tandem Topgrading interview, there are in-person meetings.

Why "Influences" during the Education Years Are Important

Early influences "stick." They mold us into who we are today. We all become hardwired early in life, so one of the first questions candidates are asked is "Through your teen years, who were major influencers (coaches, parents, or others)? And how did they influence who you are today in terms of your career goals, personality, and values?" As you go through the job history, you'll see those influences appear, some positive and some negative. Those hardwired tendencies are in us all—including your candidates—today. Some influences are positive: "Work hard …

Build relationships by asking about them." Some can interfere with career success: "Never back down … Never tell a boss no."

Ways You Can Learn Better
Interview Techniques

There are many ways to improve. Attend a workshop. (We're biased on which one.) Read books. (We're biased on those too; the second edition of *Topgrading* has a course on interviewing in it.) Observe interviewers trained in Topgrading and have them observe you and give you feedback (the most valuable part of the workshops Chris and his professionals provide). Watch YouTube videos on Topgrading interviewing. And here is one you should always use: after each interview, the first thing you should do is exchange feedback between yourself and your interview partner. You both ask, "What did I do well? And how could I improve my interview style?" This exercise will take only ten minutes, but with every interview you'll get better and better. Early on after training, the most common feedback interviewers give each other is "Smile more!" People are so conscientious about asking questions and taking notes that they frown too much. Relax and pass the baton to your interview partner if you feel yourself becoming overwhelmed.

Learn the Legal Requirements and Restrictions in Hiring, Including Interviewing

We have always consulted with legal counsel to ensure our methodology satisfies legal requirements. To our knowledge, there has never been a successful legal challenge to any part of Topgrading.[3]

The key to legal compliance is in how you, as a company, implement the methodology. Employment law varies by state and city, so we encourage you to have legal counsel review your hiring practices to ensure you are aware of, and conform to, all applicable requirements. On a federal level, many categories are "protected classes" and cannot be a factor in hiring decisions (or any other employment decision): race, color, religion, sex (including pregnancy, sexual orientation, and gender identity), national origin, age (forty or older), disability, and genetic information. As you know, employment law is fluid and constantly tested in courts of law. Topgrading methods minimize bias.

Topgrading enhances diversity, equity, and inclusion (DEI) because fairness has been embedded in the method since it was created. To begin, it minimizes bias and prejudice by *hiring based on a job scorecard, not a vague job description.* If the job requirements are not clear, it's all too easy to hire people fitting a historic stereotype. Topgrading *expands the opportunities for candidates to demonstrate competencies.* Typical interviews, which focus on too few competencies and only a few questions about each, almost always *invite* bias and prejudice. Vague conclusions about candidates result in a tendency

---

3   However, in the second edition of *Topgrading*, there is a major section on how *not* to Topgrade. The Ford Motor Company CEO rolled out a forced distribution system in which the bottom 10 percent would eventually be fired. Thirty managers sued and won. The system was not called Topgrading, and in the book we argue against such "rank-and-yank systems."

to rely on old stereotypes about how someone could succeed. The thorough, chronological Topgrading interview covers many more competencies, giving people with nontraditional backgrounds more opportunities to show outstanding competencies and to cite real examples of success in unusual circumstances. With the Topgrading interview, *all questions in the interview guide are asked of* all *candidates* (plus follow-up questions), and they are all job-related. *Conclusions are based on hard data and facts, not vague intuition.* Users of the Topgrading interview say that working with an interview partner forces conclusions based on hard data, rather than unsubstantiated intuition. Put bluntly, tandem interviewers commonly admit that their own bias is minimized because their interview partner is keeping an eye out for it. Interview partners should be from a diverse pool. It's not difficult for companies with two hundred-plus employees to have a pool of interviewers with diversity. Smaller companies can contract with diverse interviewers. And *Topgrading solves the problem of unfair bosses.* Candidates are asked to arrange reference calls with managers they've reported to and others. During the interview, candidates assess their bosses. And when candidates say that some bosses were not fair in appraising them, they are asked who else at that level would be fairer, someone they would arrange a reference call with. Just about everyone has at least one boss who is a jerk. Ditto for reference calls with peers and direct reports.

The thread running through Topgrading is thoroughness, verifiable data, hard facts, and the best opportunity for bias and prejudice to be minimized. Interviews give all candidates the opportunity to tell their complete story, starting with their education years.

A word of caution: In companies rolling out Topgrading, we've noted that all managers are trained (virtually or on-site) in two-day workshops. More than a full day is devoted to explaining twenty-

SHALLOW, UNREVEALING INTERVIEWS

four interviewing essentials, with significant practice plus feedback from a Topgrading interview expert. Having read this chapter, try the method, and you will amaze yourself with your deeper insights. But don't expect to hire almost all A Players until you learn more about interviewing and practice a lot more. Even without attending a two-day workshop, the tandem interview makes it a lot easier and a lot more revealing than going solo. You'll find the Tandem Topgrading interview, turbo-boosted with the Truth Motivator, a godsend.

Topgrading information will make onboarding smoother and help new hires be more successful. For example, we interviewed a candidate for an executive vice president role, to advise GMs throughout the world to embrace new corporate HR solutions, mainly a much more effective hiring process. She claimed every boss in the past decade would say she's a *Very Good* performer but not *Excellent*. (In fact, they did, but they also said it was a lot of work to "run interference" for her.) So, we nudged her: "If your bosses would say you were an A Player, you probably didn't have any *major* weaker points. So what will they tell us were your areas for improvement?" For every job, she admitted that she pushed people too hard, causing them to push back and making her initiatives slower to be embraced. So, this candidate is talented and gets results but can also be a pain in the neck to work with? And because too many of our clients' HR programs had mixed success, GMs were suspicious of anyone saying, "I'm from corporate; I'm here to help."

After reference checking, the candidate was hired, and the CEO insisted on her traveling the world and initially just asking questions, such as "What do you like and not like about HR policies and methods?" As the CEO and new hire anticipated, ineffective hiring was a common problem. After that "listening" tour, revisions in HR policies, including a rollout of Topgrading, were created and launched with input from the GMs and HR. In the company-feedback-survey process, she was rated high in listening and working with people.

The points of this story: (1) No one is perfect. Assume all A Players have areas for improvement. By learning a candidate's weaker points, you can try ways to minimize or even overcome them as soon as your new hire starts. (2) People can overcome weaker points when they admit they have them and embrace a plan to fix them.

Chapter Summary

- Early in our careers, the two of us experienced all the problems you experience hiring people.
- Competency interviews do some things well (address some competencies, provide structure, include same questions for all), but they have serious flaws (are too short, address too few competencies, are easily faked) that contribute to mis-hires.
- For managerial and professional individual jobs, use two interviewers to conduct the Topgrading interview.
- Follow the Topgrading interview guide for fairness, legal defensibility, thoroughness, accuracy—and better hires.
- Topgrading is a fair (DEI) hiring method.
- Topgrading Interviews can be conducted virtually.

CHAPTER 7

Hiring Problem #4—Worthless Reference Calls

Implementing the practice of requiring the candidate to arrange personal reference calls with bosses has greatly expedited and improved the quality of the reference-checking process. Talking with bosses always adds "color commentary" to assessments and confirms what candidates said in interview.

—Ken Schiller, Co-CEO, K&N Management

In this chapter, we'll review the basic problem with reference checks, discuss nuances to the solution we have already mentioned (candidate-arranged reference calls), and then explain some important ways to make your reference calls highly effective. We conclude with a hope for the future—that not just all candidates "tell the whole truth" but all companies do, too, in reference calls … and not risk getting sued.

A Review of the Basic Problem—
What You Already Know

You would love to verify what candidates have said because the most valuable information you can get about a candidate is an honest assessment of their prior performance from former managers. It's simple: performance in a similar role should provide indications about the likelihood of success in the next job.

But companies are fearful of the perceived legal risk of managers taking reference calls and the manager or the company being sued by a former employee because of negative things said about their performance or character. So, most companies discourage managers from taking reference calls, and they send people wanting reference information to HR, who will generally reveal only employment dates and job titles.

Because job seekers think you will not talk with their managers, low performers can easily hide information you need. When prospective employers ask for references, candidates list people they know will give them a glowing review—neighbors, friends, and friendly business associates. But they rarely include the managers they reported to, the people best equipped to describe the performance-related competencies that are so crucial for you to know. Your experience is that reference calls are typically worthless, and recent research shows, more and more, companies have given up on reference calls. Why go through the motions? Why? Because there are solutions.

You already know that the Truth Motivator is restated at the beginning of the Topgrading interview. And you know that during the Topgrading interview for every job, the candidate is asked, "How would your manager, Amy Adams, rate your performance if we ask you to arrange a call with her?" The guesses are amazingly accurate.

We know this because clients have reported for the past four decades that when they talk with bosses, the guesses by the candidate turn out to be spot on. Of course! It would be foolish for a candidate to claim that Amy would rate their performance *Excellent* when they know the rating would likely be lower.

Hiring Solution #4: Conduct Candidate-Arranged Reference Calls

Having the candidate set up the reference calls after completing the Tandem Topgrading interview has been eye-opening. Candidates know up front that they will be arranging these calls and they tend to be open and honest during the interview process because of it. We have not had any big surprises in any of the reference calls we have done.

—Larry Sheftel, Director of Human Resources, MDI Group

There are many reasons to actually do the reference calls. The #1 reason is to understand how candidates performed in each job and what their boss felt about them. To make the point, if you *hypothetically* used the Truth Motivator and only had twenty minutes for an interview, you could ask several boss-related questions and get extremely valuable insights:

1. Ask the candidate to appraise *the strengths and weaker points of each boss*. As the hiring manager, do you fit the pattern of what the candidate likes in a boss? We have interviewed candidates who were highly critical of every manager they reported to, using words like "jerk," "idiot," "incompetent,"

etc. Would you like to be the next manager they describe in that manner?

2. Ask your candidate how bosses would rate *the candidate's overall performance* (*Excellent, Very Good, Good, Fair, Poor*).

3. Ask what their bosses would list as *the candidate's strengths and weaker points*.

Wow! You'd have a treasure trove of essential information (but of course don't cut Topgrading Interviews to 20 minutes)!

How to Conduct Candidate-Arranged Reference Calls

At the appropriate time, usually when a job offer is being discussed, give the list of bosses and others you want to talk with to your candidate. "And others" means this: You have heard about peers and direct reports as the candidate described various jobs. For a managerial job, include reference calls with some of them. Ask for A Player peers and direct reports because A Players will provide more valid opinions and insights than weaker performers will share. You don't want to be influenced by a lazy C Player who hates a boss (your candidate) because said boss required better performance.

Typically, you would ask the managerial candidate to arrange calls with about eight people—four bosses, two peers, two direct reports. For a sales rep candidate, five (three sales managers, two customers). For a cashier, three (all five-minute calls with former managers).

In many companies, there is not a written policy forbidding taking reference calls—just a caution to managers that it's probably not smart to tell a reference that a former employee was fired for poor performance. The good news is this: managers of former A Players almost always take reference calls, and if there is a written policy prohibiting them doing so, they ignore it. They figure that there is zero chance, if they say anything negative about the former A Player, they or the company will get sued. *In fact, we are unaware of any lawsuit having anything to do with Topgrading, ever. And we have never heard of any managers getting into trouble for taking a reference call.* Managers of former A Players figure that taking the call is the right thing to do and no one will care. If the former employee was a C Player, former bosses are more apt to decline to take the call, explaining, "It's against company policy." It's more likely that the C Player candidate, knowing they will probably not get former bosses to talk, will drop out early in the hiring process. Good!

Over the years, we've noticed a trend for companies to not actually have a policy prohibiting managers from accepting reference calls. "Discouraging" the calls is becoming more widespread, perhaps because so many managers are willing to take calls regarding former A Players and no one seems to get into trouble. And, as you will read, in many states companies and managers are protected from such lawsuits.

To be clear, candidates do not actually schedule reference calls. You tell the candidate to ask the reference if they'd be willing to take your call and, if so, "At what number? And when is convenient in the next couple of days?" Candidates will typically get back to you within forty-eight hours and say, "Yes, all the people you want to talk to are willing. I'll email their phone numbers and availability." If a candidate does not call back within three days with permission granted by almost all the intended references, that's a red flag!

How to Ask Candidates to Ask Former Managers to Take Reference Calls without Violating Their Company Policy

If a reference works in a company with a "take no reference calls" policy, clients have discovered ways around it. According to clients, it's rare for a finalist candidate to say, "I tried to arrange a call with Pat, but she said, 'Sorry, it's against company policy,' so all you can do is ask HR for my employment information." Although almost all managers do accept reference calls when asked by a former A Player, if you hear, "It's against company policy," here are solutions:

1. **Tell the candidate to request a *personal* reference call (discussing character, values, etc.).** Most "don't accept reference calls" policies prohibit *business* reference calls (discussing jobs, performance); personal calls (discussing character, values) are permissible. Focusing on personal attributes will still reveal important competencies.

2. **Ask the candidate to get permission for the call.** Suggest to the candidate that their reference go to HR or another top executive and say, "Hey, HR, Tammy Smith was an A Player for us for eight years, left three years ago, and now is asking me to serve as a reference. I want to do it because someday I hope she will rejoin us."

3. **Ask the candidate to request a reference call with a *peer* of the boss.** Maybe that person will be willing to talk.

4. **Ask the candidate to arrange a call with someone who has left the company.** They are not bound by the company policy on reference calls.

5. **At the extreme, if the candidate refuses to arrange reference calls until accepting your job offer, agree!** But make the offer contingent upon "no surprises" in the reference calls. So, your candidate is now a new hire, and if reference calls make you regret hiring the person, you can legally fire them. The good news is this never happens (to our knowledge). And here's why: the new hire, as a candidate, did not hide weaker points, and the bosses did not disclose any new, serious weaker points.

A very common offshoot of #5 is a verbal promise and handshake: "I will offer you the job if the reference calls do not reveal anything that convinces me to not offer the job." This works well because, at that point in the selection process, a high level of trust has been generated, almost all reference calls have been conducted (with no "red flags" popping up), and that final reference call is just a formality.

Push candidates to get people to talk to you, but if, for example, only two out of seven intended references agree, hiring the person is risky.

Focus on the Most Recent Decade

Most of our clients want to talk with bosses for all jobs in the most recent decade. They figure that even if the person had significant weaker points and mixed job performance prior to the past ten years, it probably isn't relevant now. Probably not. But at the senior manager level, you want to be sure. You've conducted a Topgrading interview covering all jobs, and you've heard what all bosses would say were the candidate's successes, mistakes, and overall performance. You have also heard details of accomplishments (and mistakes) and heard names, not only of bosses but of peers and direct reports. If you want some reference calls with anyone prior to the most recent decade, go ahead and ask.

For Management and Professional Jobs, the Topgrading Interviewers Typically Conduct Reference Calls Either Solo or Together

After all, both tandem interviewers heard the candidate describe what they like and do not like about their managers and guessed how their managers would rate their performance in a reference call. It saves time when both tandem interviewers conduct solo reference calls. But to delegate these important verification calls to someone in HR—someone who hardly knows the candidate, let alone the reference, someone who was not a tandem interviewer—will produce vague information. The HR person will probably sound like a customer service representative reading from a script—leading to the reference, not feeling much trust, to be inclined to just give some positive platitudes.

In preparation to conduct reference calls, you and your interview partner review all your notes about the job: the job scorecard, phone screen interview notes, and Topgrading interview notes. And if you haven't, talk to those who conducted the phone screen interview if it wasn't you.

Then conduct the reference calls. A common format:

Hi, Richard. Pat said you're willing to talk with me as a reference. Thank you for your willingness. Is this a good time?

If so ...

Please tell me about Pat's job—approximate dates, job title, responsibilities, and how Pat did (how you rate Pat's performance).

What were Pat's strengths, assets, things you liked about Pat's performance, and things Pat did well?

We all have areas for improvement. What were Pat's weaker points and areas for improvement?

Let me tell you about the job we have open, and then, if you will, comment on how well you think Pat would fit in it.

Now is the time to check for the specific weaker points you learned about in the Tandem Topgrading interview.

Pat said you might be a bit critical of his personal organization. How did that affect Pat's overall performance?

Ask about any other concerns or weaker points. This is powerful! Although references of A Players tend to be honest and reveal some weaker points, they also tend to be generous with praise and stingy on weaker points. This is normal. Remember, all A Players have weaker points, but their strengths far outweigh them. So the reference source is apt to think, "Of course I'll highlight the strengths." Here's the point. As soon as you point out a *real* weaker point that has not been mentioned, that reference will immediately be more forthcoming, thinking, "Holy cow, this prospective boss really knows [candidate], so my ignoring some weaker points won't help [candidate] get the job."

The vast majority of the calls are extremely positive. Sure, bosses of A Players will say glowing things but not because they are trying to manipulate you into hiring the candidate; it's because the candidate is that good! You'll be surprised when references do list candidates' weaker points and areas for improvement. They typically say, "[Candidate] knows I'll probably mention these." But they also say things like, "We all have weaker points. [Candidate] worked to minimize them, and I mention these within context as [candidate's] performance was excellent overall."

The most value comes late in each reference call, after you've built rapport and trust. You'll get hints as to how to best onboard and motivate the candidate and learn about any idiosyncrasies you'll be glad to know about (and maybe avoid some embarrassment). You should promise confidentiality, but don't overpromise. Say you want to be able to share the substance of reference calls with others—maybe HR and other managers who will interact a lot with the candidate. It would be difficult to swear everyone to secrecy. Topgraders have a good sense of professionalism and instinctively know that reference calls should remain private—shared only on a need-to-know basis.

Should Businesses Permit, or Even Encourage, Managers to Take Reference Calls? (A Plea Mostly to CEOs)

It's too bad that fears of lawsuits scare companies into prohibiting managers from taking reference calls! Just think of how beneficial it would be if managers in all companies routinely took reference calls and told the truth, including details of why a low performer was fired. The current mass mutual charade—candidates fudging to get jobs and companies discouraging managers from taking reference calls—hurts every company, including yours, if you prohibit or discourage managers from taking reference calls. And the charade hurts high performers who can lose out in job searches to candidates who game the system. With more than half of all hires turning out to be disappointments, our economy is "damaged goods."

Forgive us for taking you on a short intellectual journey to describe a *big* potential solution to the problem of dishonesty—of candidates fooling you in order to get hired. Here is something you probably don't know. Depending on where you are located, you and your company are probably not at much risk if you take reference calls, even if you say truthful negative statements about former employees. As long as managers provide honest feedback about the employee and their performance, there is less risk in providing a reference than in almost any other employment action. In fact, the vast majority of states have laws that *give employers immunity for providing truthful information regarding former employees, even negative performance appraisals.* In the US, we've created this "don't ask, don't tell" environment when it comes to references, even when there's minimal risk. Isn't business essentially about assessing and managing risk? We take risks in business every day, but we can't be paralyzed by every conceptual risk that may be out there. And we all would benefit from more informative, honest employment references.

> As long as managers provide honest feedback about the employee and their performance, there is less risk in providing a reference than in almost any other employment action.

Ironically, the people who are most punished by the widespread failure to provide honest, informative reference calls are our *best* former employees. These are employees who want their former managers to sing their praises, lament the fact that they decided to leave, and tell the prospective employer that they would happily bring the candidate back to their company.

Bottom line: you have rarely received the straight scoop on candidates—you've been fooled by many—because you didn't talk with their bosses. Unfortunately, your company is partially to blame. If your company doesn't permit managers to take reference calls, why should other companies? Some companies *are* leading the way toward the *big* solution.

Culligan Encourages Managers to Take Reference Calls

Scott Clawson, CEO of Culligan Water, not only permits but *encourages* managers to take reference calls and speak the truth about former employees' strengths and their weaker points. As Scott put it, "It's the fair thing to do. Low performers should either perform better, get better with training and coaching, transfer into jobs where they could be an A Player, or resign. It's not fair to their future employers for our managers not to tell the truth about their performance to get jobs they'll fail at."

Scott has an advantage. He doesn't worry about lawsuits from disgruntled former employees because almost 90 percent of the people hired at Culligan turn out to be A Players; there are almost no fired employees. Topgrading companies do what Scott just described (but few allow their managers to take reference calls). They Topgrade in ways you've learned. They nail down accountabilities, in job scorecards, before someone is hired; provide feedback, training, and coaching to help people meet those accountabilities; and are very clear that people failing to achieve agreed-upon goals will have to move into another job in the company, where they can perform at the A Player level or leave the company. Employees who know they will not be able to achieve the measurable goals they agreed to, and who cannot move into another job at the company, quietly find another job and resign … and there is a nice going-away party at lunch. With that sort of honesty, integrity, and fairness in company policies, baseless lawsuits are almost unthinkable.

Considering Culligan's experience, and the fact that truthful references are substantially protected, changing the paradigm on employment references nationally would be a win-win for all businesses and for the A Players who make our business run. If and when most businesses permit/encourage managers to take reference calls, Topgrading companies will probably be among the first to do so. There's nothing like hiring almost all high performers to make possible reference checks a nonissue.

Reference Check Laws

Just as you must know how all the federal, state, and local laws affect hiring in your location, you should remain informed about laws governing reference calls, even reference calls candidates arrange. To find out what the laws are in each state, we have found this resource to be helpful: https://www.nolo.com/legal-encyclopedia/free-books/employee-rights-book/chapter9-6.html.

For example, at the time this book went to press, this resource showed the law in Illinois to be as follows:

Illinois. 745 Ill. Comp. Stat. § 46/10.

Information that may be disclosed: job performance

Who may request or receive information: prospective employer

Employer immune from liability: (if) information is truthful

Employer immune from liability unless: information is knowingly false or in violation of a civil right

Thousands of claims and lawsuits are filed against employers by former employees every year, yet a tiny percent of them are related to references provided to prospective employers. One reason, of course, is that not many managers are willing to take reference calls. Most of those suits are not about information provided to the prospective employer; they're about information *not* provided to the prospective employer when there might have been a duty to provide that information. More importantly, the legal basis for almost all reference check claims is defamation; a claim that can only be proven if the information provided was knowingly false or was provided without regard to the truth. In other words, avoid taking "revenge" reference calls; stick to the facts, and the former employee has no valid claim.

In our highly litigious society, it's unlikely that the norm will change so that (all) companies will allow their managers to take reference calls and even be specific about why an employee was fired.

In the meantime, enjoy your competitive advantage if *you* conduct candidate-arranged reference calls with bosses—and competitors don't! You will use the Truth Motivator. You will have conducted Tandem Topgrading Interviews that reveal everything job-relevant about dozens of competencies, and you will have taken thorough notes about candidates who told you about every job and what bosses felt about their performance. Since you have finalist candidates who are very willing to arrange reference calls with the people you want to talk with, you have a solution—not *the big* solution but a proven solution, foolproof hiring. It's candidate-arranged reference calls.

Chapter Summary

- Conduct candidate-arranged reference calls with bosses and others when the candidate is willing (usually when a job offer is being discussed).
- Focus on the most recent decade, though if there were problems prior to that, talk to some people about the candidate's earlier career history.
- Expect candidates to arrange calls with 90 percent of the people with whom you want to talk.
- If references balk at arranging calls, change the purpose to "personal," not "a business call"; ask HR permission; talk to people who have left the company; or make the job offer contingent upon no surprises when the reference calls are made (even after you hire the person).
- Check your state and local laws to be sure you're protected.
- For the future think, "If we build talent methods as Culligan has done, maybe we should not just permit but encourage managers to take reference calls, even when the former employee was a poor performer."

CHAPTER 8

Hiring Problem #5— Applicant-Screening Tools Don't Work

This chapter begins with a critique of some traditional employment tests and the current fad to us—AI-assisted applicant-screening tools. It finishes with the results of years of research that produced the Topgrading screening tool the PreScreen Snapshot—a remarkably simple tool created to avoid all the problems with the other hiring tools. Ironically, the PreScreen Snapshot actually assures improved validity of personality tests because it eliminates candidates most likely to fake personality tests.

As explained in chapter 4 ("Not Enough Applicants"), unless you are using top-flight, highly targeted internal or external recruiters, your Topgrading success is highly correlated with the number of applicants you generate. If you receive only five résumés, the chances of hiring a high performer are slim; if you get twenty or fifty résumés, you increase your odds of hiring an A Player—if you have an effective screening tool.

For the vast majority of companies, here is the quandary. If you get so many résumés that you *must* use some sort of applicant-screening tool to reduce the pool of applicants you can pursue, how do you choose among the hundreds of tests and screening tools? Almost all of them, despite their slick marketing, are deeply flawed. And even the most "proven" long tests, used after screening—tests with complex technical manuals "proving" solid validity and reliability—are a mixed bag. Some (ability and knowledge tests, games, simulations) can be used with confidence to help you hire people with relevant skills. But most of the "proven" tests aren't so proven, and the vast majority of screening tools simply do not work. Testing for businesses is a multibillion-dollar industry. In this chapter, we focus mostly on applicant-screening tools but also cover the big, old employment-testing industry, because they want you to be their customer. This chapter is a bit technical, but if you want to use "validated" tests or AI-assisted screening tools, please read it carefully, and you'll hire better than if you use the wrong tests. In this chapter, you'll learn about the following:

- The current state of traditional "legitimate" employment testing to help you avoid hiring mistakes;
- The avalanche of AI-assisted screening tools that are seriously flawed, for reasons solid academic research has spelled out (and you can read); and
- The solution—the PreScreen Snapshot, a simple two-job form, a tool that really does identify the best applicants without the many problems that come with using conventional tests and AI-assisted tools.

Don't take our word for the critique of various instruments. It's tacky to take potshots at the competition, so we will show you articles written by experts. Here are compelling, authoritative articles:

1. **Legal Issues Relating to Pre-Employment Testing (Criteria Corp)**

   https://www.criteriacorp.com/resources/defin-itive-guide-validity-of-preemployment-tests/legal-issues-relating-pre-employment

   Tests have to conform to Uniform Guidelines Governing Pre-Employment Testing (UGESP), which informs decisions by the Equal Employment Occupation Commission (EEOC). Tests of course should be job-related and not discriminate on the basis of age, sex, race, religion, disabilities, etc.

2. **Your Hiring Assessments Could Get You in Trouble, Society for Human Resources Management (SHRM)**

   https://www.shrm.org/resourcesandtools/hr-topics/talent-acquisition/pages/your-hiring-assessments-could-get-you-in-trouble.aspx

   Organizational psychologists are quoted saying many tests claim to identify the best candidates but fail to do so.

3. **Stop Screening Job Candidates' Social Media, *Harvard Business Review***

   https://hbr.org/2021/09/stop-screening-job-candidates-social-media

   You're not supposed to discriminate against people in certain categories, but a significant share of profiles contain information that companies may be legally prohibited from

131

considering, including gender, race, and ethnicity (all evident in 100 percent of profiles), disabilities (7 percent), pregnancy status (3 percent), sexual orientation (59 percent), political views (21 percent), and religious affiliation (41 percent). Many of the job seekers' profiles also included information of potential concern to prospective employers: 51 percent of them contained profanity, 11 percent gave indications of gambling, 26 percent showed or referenced alcohol consumption, and 7 percent referenced drug use. Even if you can legally get away with accessing such information, do you really want to do it?

4. **Ethics of AI-Enabled Recruiting and Selection: A Review and Research Agenda,** *Springer*

https://link.springer.com/article/10.1007/s10551-022-05049-6

This is a meta-study that focused on fifty-one scientific studies. They show the theoretical promise of AI-assisted tools plus the many ways they fail to live up to their promise. The last article could be a doctoral dissertation, with fifty-one studies summarized, with references to hundreds of academically published sources. This meta-research covers the landscape of testing research and ends with dozens of suggestions to, put bluntly, clean up the huge mess that can cause you mis-hires today.

To put this in perspective, sure, use ability and knowledge tests to help you hire people with job-relevant skills, but be sure they don't discriminate against protected groups.

Brief History of Testing in Business

If you use or might use any of the well-established hiring tests, you really should know a bit about their history. Testing candidates goes back four thousand years, with rulers and military officers wanting to select Rambos. During WWI, the US military had hundreds of psychologists developing a huge variety of tests (intelligence, physical endurance, resilience under pressure, and specialized aptitude tests related to the technical fields, such as mechanical ability,

Sure, use ability and knowledge tests to help you hire people with job-relevant skills, but be sure they don't discriminate against protected groups.

electrical knowledge, and, later, electronics). There are also clerical and administrative tests, simulations, leadership games, radio code operational tests, language tests, and driver-selection tests, etc. The combinations are endless. A complex series of tests was administered to candidates for every job in the military using each branch of the military's "classification" test. Naturally, armies (sorry for the pun) of military psychologists, after WWII, went into companies, transitioning the tests to civilian jobs. They created "batteries" of tests and simulations that in business are called *assessment centers*. A big testing industry was born, and dozens of major universities launched undergraduate and graduate programs with major emphasis on testing.

Brad's Story (Continued)

*My master's and doctoral programs emphasized testing. I was dis-
appointed. In the real world, I found that many personality tests
didn't predict whether a person would become a high performer;
I found the testing validation manuals were usually deceptive,
and, indeed, some actually eliminated as many high performers
as low performers. During the 1970s, 1980s, and 1990s, dozens of
new tests, called "nonmilitary employment tests," were created.
Employment tests were typically administered on site after applicants had been screened. We joined the trend by "testing the
tests" for clients. And we ran assessment centers with three or
four days of tests, interviews, simulations, group decision-making
exercises, speeches, and mock performance reviews. Profession-
ally, in addition to assessing candidates for executive jobs and
coaching them, we validated assessment center individual tests
... until they proved to be just fads.*

*Bottom line, after running about fifty assessment centers our
research showed they were too time consuming, expensive, and
wasteful. Only one component identified which managers who
were assessed and then promoted, would turn out to be high performers. Can you guess which one? The interview, early versions of
the Topgrading interview. We saved clients time and money when
we showed that just using the Topgrading interview identified
future high performers very well, and adding all the other results
of simulations, role-plays, etc., added no improvement in predict-
ing success. Nada.*

*Cutting to the chase: ability, knowledge, and interest tests—admin-
istered and used properly—are useful and not discriminatory. But*

popular personality tests are easily faked and the tests we properly validated were worthless, or even harmful.

And while we're being critical of certain tests … Caution: Two properly researched and developed tests are often used for hiring but *should not be.* The Myers-Briggs Type Indicator (MBTI) is fine for coaching and team building but not for hiring; it was not created to be used for hiring. The Minnesota Multiphasic Personality Inventory (MMPI) is designed to identify psychological disorders and should only be used appropriately, such as for screening candidates for police officers on their emotional stability.

Today many large companies have teams of psychologists who are up to date on innovations. They validate tests within the company. The test providers offer "off-the-shelf" tests to companies to use without having to do internal validation, as long as they could show relevance to the job and follow Equal Employment Opportunity Commission (EEOC) rules. For example, a typing test used to screen candidates for typist jobs is likely to be judged appropriately for typing jobs in other companies, but not for screening candidates for truck drivers. Another caution: all test users (that means you, too) must keep a careful eye on possible adverse impacts—meaning if you use scorable off-the-shelf tests and if cutoff scores systematically reject members of any protected group, complaints or legal actions might occur.

Applicant-screening tools are intended to narrow the funnel from many candidates to a few who will be phone screened and then invited to participate in further hiring steps. Applicants balk at spending more than fifteen minutes being screened before they get to talk to a real human (not just a "friendly" bot). If your company is named Tesla, Amazon, or Goldman Sachs, applicants willingly go through extensive hoops before talking to someone. Various employment tests can be added to screen out most applicants if your company is an "employer of choice." There are literally thousands of products that use AI to help human resources do just about everything, and hundreds of applicant-screening tools are on the market promising better hiring, but as the articles cited above show, there are huge problems associated with using them.

What You Need to Know About Validity

We apologize for introducing something that is confusing but important if you want to use conventional tests or scorable screening tools. There are clever scams in the testing industry, making it easy for users to be conned. All tests should be "valid," right? The following paragraphs will help you not be fooled.

The attention, historically, has been on conventional tests, and dozens of them have been validated and revalidated. And to repeat, many are useful. But in our experience, many cheat in the following ways:

- **Implying that a test improves hiring success (but does not) because "validation showed it is reliable."** Do you think a proven reliable test will "reliably" improve Quality of Hire? Not at all! Reliability in testing is shown when alternate forms of the test (or every other item) have scores that are highly cor-related. So, if you just take the odd items and get a score and then take the even items and get a score, the scores will be very similar. But you could use a "reliable" test that *fails to improve hiring at all*, because although the even and odd items on basket-weaving knowledge (or whatever) do correlate, basket weaving may not be at all relevant to the job.

- **Implying that a test improves hiring (but does *not*) because it has "face validity."** All that means is that test takers see that the items all on basket weaving (or whatever) relate to the job of weaving baskets (or whatever).

- **Implying that the test improves hiring (but does not) because it has "construct validity."** All that means is that regardless of the test's face validity, it has been proven that the basket-weaving test truly measures what it is supposed to measure (basket weaving).

- **Saying that the test shows predictive validity, when it doesn't significantly improve Quality of Hire.** All the test developer has to do is validate it with thousands of subjects. With a large N, if the test improves hiring high performers from 25 percent to 25.1 percent, it demonstrates predictive validity—but without any practical improvement in hiring.

Bottom line: the "technical manuals" of many tests say the test is reliable and has demonstrated face validity, construct validity, and (most important) predictive validity, but we've never seen a technical manual showing meaningful improvement hiring high performers.

Irony of Ironies: Topgrading Has the Potential to Improve the Predictive Validity of Personality Tests

We've said a problem with tests in general and particularly personality tests is that they can be faked or "right answers" can be found online. What if there was a way of determining who are the honest test takers versus the fakers? Surely the personality profiles of those who take the test honestly are apt to be more real, more valid. The Topgrading Truth Motivator, administered at the beginning of the application process, does it. The PreScreen Snapshot uses the Truth Motivator!

Do Not Believe "Experts" Who Say Past Work Experiences Do Not Predict Future Performance

Forbes magazine ran an article titled "Hiring and Recruitment Trends to Expect in 2022." The author, a CEO of a company selling skills testing and behavioral assessment, stated, "Next up on our list of emerging recruiting trends is the use of advanced screening tools. While skills tests and other evaluation tools have been around for decades, quite a few organizations still screen candidates by reviewing résumés and conducting interviews. While these tactics certainly have their merits, they do not provide quantifiable data about candidates' skills and abilities."

We beg to differ! Topgrading gets you honest, thorough, verifiable accounts of how a candidate performed in every job—what their major successes and mistakes were, how the person was rated by every manager, what the person liked and disliked about each job, and what sort of cultures they did well in—and you can verify everything the candidate told you with candidate-arranged reference calls. So, *past performance can be an outstanding predictor of next-job performance.* It's only true that "reviewing résumés and conducting interviews" produces lousy hiring results when the major hiring problems have not been solved. Indeed, we show that when the main hiring problems are solved, the results are better than with any other method.

Testing and Screening Tools That Are Common and Incur Minimal Legal Risks

As you know, anyone in the US can sue anyone for any reason, good or bad, merited or not. Having an employment lawyer check your hiring methods could be insurance. An employment lawyer might caution you on the topic of "adverse impact."

- **Study an applicant's résumé and the company's application form (or career history form).** Fortunately, certain applicant-screening tools are commonly used, make sense, and are rarely challenged legally. Application forms, like résumés, when they are not scored and are interpreted by human beings (not bots), are the most common traditional means to screen people.

- **Use "knockout questions" in the application process.** If the job is virtual or on location, you might ask which are acceptable. If the job is in the Arctic Circle, asking if the applicant is willing to move there can save both you and the applicant time. Asking knockout questions is usually effective, but don't include more than three knockout questions, or candidates will balk.

- **Conduct structured phone screen interviews.** Standard, job-related questions cut the pool of applicants down to those who will be asked to go through the company's hiring processes (tests, interviews, etc.), at the company's location or virtually.

- **Administer employment tests, properly created and properly used.** These include ability tests (typing, programming); knowledge tests (law); simulations of real-life situations on the job (waiting tables, trial law, coaching a failing employee); and some personality tests, which, we repeat, can finally be accurate and useful because the PreScreen Snapshot identifies people not likely to fudge the test.

Why AI-Assisted Applicant-Screening Tools Are Criticized

The influx of AI-assisted hiring tools is like a hiring pandemic. If your applicant-screening tool is worthless, the candidates you interview will not include many high performers.

- As you can read article #4 (above), AI-assisted applicant-screening tools have not (yet) been shown to improve hiring high performers, and many suffer from bias and adverse impact. You can read how Amazon was found guilty of discriminating against women using such tools.

- Many are accused of violating a series of federal laws. (One of many is Title VII of the Civil Rights Act, decisions by the EEOC.)

- Some bots scan people's social media posts, so there is a huge risk that information that is illegal to ask for (race, religion, pregnancy, etc.) will influence hiring. How can anyone hiring ignore the information that you can't legally ask candidates about? Even if some court says companies can scan social media with little legal risk, would you want to do it?

- Research has identified algorithms that—get this—systematically overlook the most qualified applicants.

- Facial recognition and voice recognition is AI-assisted, with horror stories of bias. The EEOC has ruled that video interviews are legal—even though it's easy to guess age, gender, race, etc.—as long as the same questions are asked of all candidates, because the value of the answers outweighs bias that might occur by seeing what people look like. Hmm … Do these last two bullet points put your mind at ease? You shouldn't discriminate against people because of their religion, gender, etc., but maybe it's legal for you to know these things on social media or video interviews?

- Auto-sending résumés, based on keywords and "one-click apply," has made it too easy for people to apply for jobs for which they are unqualified. (And it's time consuming for you to review and delete their résumés.)

- Bots have shown to be too restrictive. They can eliminate far too many candidates. They have been instructed to reject candidates based on rigid criteria, without considering whether exceeding one criterion might more than make up for being slightly low on another. Diversity complaints are common because some AI-assisted screening tools reinforce stereotypes and bias, systematically reducing diversity.

- Most AI algorithms are kept secret. ("It's proprietary so no competitor can steal it.") Hiring methods should all be transparent and credible to applicants—and "job-related," as legally required. Candidates expect to be screened on their résumé, interview responses, tests that obviously measure necessary skills, and reference checks. But an algorithm can be a total mystery. What does the bot consider important? In Europe, hiring must legally include human judgment. It's becoming an issue in the US.

- Hiring methods should assure "informed consent" of candidates. In Europe, candidates must be told what tests, interviews, etc., they will have to take, and they must agree. How can anyone "agree" to be screened by a bot with a secret algorithm?

- AI-assisted tools can be circumvented by applicants with a carefully crafted résumé. Articles in business magazines have actually advised candidates on how to "game" the bots. ("Study the company website to find keywords. Pack your résumé with them, but don't overdo it.")

- Ability and knowledge tests (AI assisted or not) can be taken by friends online. Culture-fit tests are easily faked. (Check out the company values on their website, and complete the culture test professing those values.)

- In short, a massive testing industry exists to trick candidates into revealing things they don't want to reveal. But isn't it better to screen in candidates who want to tell you the full truth?

New Hiring Methods Are Inevitable

Just as AI-assisted hiring might one day significantly improve the percent of high performers hired, and *because hiring methods have been pathetic in business*, creative companies are pushing the reset button.

Tony Hsieh, the former CEO of Zappos (now deceased), hired way too many people, paid them for six weeks of training and assessment, kept the best, and fired the rest (with a $2,000 going-away present). Wow! He said he used such an expensive, time-consuming approach because common hiring methods were so pathetically poor.

Elon Musk and Google have an extremely innovative approach to hiring. They tell the world that those expensive college degrees are *not* necessary and experience in a job might *not* be necessary either. The employment testers have known for decades that college grades are feeble predictors of career success, but companies request that information in application forms. And the pandemic showed that traditional ways of doing jobs have to be replaced by new, flexible methods. Why hire sales reps with fifteen years of experience if they will have to unlearn old, somewhat ineffective methods? *Fast Company* found that sales reps with no experience outperformed experienced reps ten to one.

So, what is the Musk/Google "approach"? Would you believe— even with *no college* and *no program management experience*—train yourself online (for free) in program management, take tests, earn a certificate, and get a job at hundreds of companies that respect the Google Project Management Certificate. The free course is available through Coursera.

Those completing the certificate get a job in project management. The theory is this: *Instead of assuming that parroting answers from a college text predicts career success (it doesn't) and assuming work experience may not predict success, why not see how candidates do in actual, real-life learning situations—where aptitude, creativity, leadership, planning, verbal skills, decision-making, and motivation are demonstrated in project plans and confirmed in tests?*

What an interesting commentary on the current state of hiring. The best that companies can come up with is to hire people who trained themselves in some basics and to ignore traditional hiring methods! We understand and agree with this self-certification method … unless you're willing to try the methods in this book.

Hiring Solution #6: Use the Topgrading PreScreen Snapshot

The PreScreen Snapshot is amazing! Even before you talk with candidates, you've saved 50 percent screening time, and, more importantly, you know how recent bosses rate their job performance. And we conduct fewer phone screens with better candidates.

—Scott Clawson, CEO, Culligan Water

One hundred forty-eight people saw our job ad on Indeed. Sixty-four of them completed a PreScreen Snapshot. We looked at the sixty-four PreScreen Snapshots, decided who to phone screen, and offered one of them the job without having to read the other eighty-four résumés. It saved us hours, and we focused our time on the best candidates.

—Savanna Collazo, Administrative Director, MOEbiz

143

Did the first part of this chapter depress you? We can certainly relate to that feeling. Clients have been asking us to develop a really good applicant-screening tool, and in 2010 we launched the PreScreen Snapshot. It worked very well, but it was embedded in our full software—Topgrading Online Solutions (TOLS)—making it inaccessible unless you bought an annual license for the full platform. After much more work than you might think, we've extracted PreScreen Snapshot so that anyone can try it free and use it to fill one job or get a license if they would like to use it for all jobs.

> **The PreScreen Snapshot doesn't suffer from all the problems and risks of AI-assisted screening tools.**

To begin, the PreScreen Snapshot doesn't suffer from all the problems and risks of AI-assisted screening tools. After you read about it, go back to that long list of AI problems, and you'll see the PreScreen Snapshot conforms with federal and state laws (with no legal challenges we're aware of).

- It does not snoop around in applicants' social media.
- It has no bias-prone voice or facial recognition.
- It does *not* systematically eliminate the best candidates.
- It is almost impossible to be "gamed."
- It has no secret algorithm with secret ways applicants are picked.
- It has informed consent. (If an applicant doesn't want to fill out the two-job form, they don't.)
- And instead of some bot picking applicants to continue the hiring process, real humans make the judgments.

Unlike tests with "lie indicators" that don't work well, the Topgrading Truth Motivator takes away that criticism. Candidates who are willing to arrange calls with bosses almost never lie when estimating boss ratings. In a real sense, it's the world's shortest applicant form, covering only two jobs, so it has "face validity."

The PreScreen Snapshot simply asks applicants to take about eight minutes to provide information about their two most recent jobs. That's it! You don't have to do anything except make a few simple choices as to what optional questions you want to add and then send links to applicants. Candidates get a message saying, "Thank you for your interest in [job title] position at [company name]. We would like to continue the hiring process. Please use the link below to provide a little information about your two most recent jobs."

Then you start getting PreScreen Snapshots, from just the best applicants. The unique, powerful magic begins with the Truth Motivator and ends with the best verification of what candidates tell you—calls *they* arrange with their managers. (So there is no phone tag.)

As you will see below, candidates are alerted to the Truth Motivator when completing the PreScreen Snapshot.

Here is what applicants see before they begin: "Note: A final step in the hiring process is for candidates to arrange reference calls with managers. This will only be done when candidates are willing to arrange the calls (usually when a job offer is being discussed)."

Two-thirds of applicants don't complete the PreScreen Snapshot—those with hyped résumés and those not really interested in your job. Perfect! You'll be tempted to call some candidates who declined to provide information about their two most recent jobs, but you'll soon learn it's a waste of time. Most will not accept your invitation to talk, and those who do, when you remind them of the Truth Motivator, will say, "I can't get bosses to talk with you. Goodbye." What they mean is their résumé has fiction, and they don't want you to talk with their managers who might say their performance was not so hot.

> *The quality of people who show up for the initial interview is definitely higher when we use the PreScreen Snapshot. They took a little time to apply, they know what job they applied for, and there is just more engagement.*
>
> **—Gary Teuscher, Recruiter, Midtown Home Improvements**

> *The PreScreen Snapshots definitely identify top candidates. Every candidate we have hired using the PreScreen Snapshot completed it immediately and without having to be asked twice.*
>
> **—Danielle Robinson, Topgrading Director, Sport Clips**

Applicants completing the PreScreen Snapshot have already shown they are comfortable with the Truth Motivator. You just cut screening time by half because you don't have to review all the B and C Player résumés, making hiring faster. *And* you know who the most honest, high-performing one-third are. Ta-da! Problem #2 (applicants fooling you) is solved.

Additional Benefits of Using the PreScreen Snapshot

- **Your interviews are much more revealing.** The PreScreen Snapshot software generates a structured Phone Screen Interview Guide, auto-loaded with the information the candidate supplied. Because the Truth Motivator works, instead of half your applicants fooling you, it will be refreshing when your interviewees admit not just accomplishments and successes but their mistakes and weaker points too (rather than hiding them). This goes for phone screen interviews and whatever other interviews you conduct. (Hopefully you'll use the Topgrading interview.) They all are instantly more revealing interviews because, again, your interviewees are forthcoming, and again, because they know they'll eventually have to arrange reference calls with their bosses. Problem #3 (unrevealing interviews) is partially solved! However, you probably still need to improve your interviewing skills to completely solve it.

- **Reference calls with bosses are easy.** You don't have to ask candidates if it's OK if *they* arrange reference calls as a final step in hiring; the fact they filled out the PreScreen Snapshot shows they are happy to arrange the calls. Problem #4 (poor validation) is solved.

- **Personality test results are more accurate.** Why? The one-third of applicants completing the two-job questions read the instructions, embraced the Truth Motivator, and are not inclined to game the test.

- **PreScreen Snapshot is a screening tool that works.** It doesn't solve the problem of "not enough applicants," but it identifies the best one-third of your applicants, and problem #5 (weak screening tools) is solved.

Using the PreScreen Snapshot, I save about sixteen hours every time I fill an open position and get much better candidates.

—Nyisha Moore, Director of Human Resources, Automation X

Below is a sample PreScreen Snapshot. If you choose to ask for salary history (which is prohibited in certain states and cities), this Snapshot is what you will see. If not, the graph will instead highlight estimated performance ratings. Please take a minute to study this, and be sure to focus on *Reason for Leaving* and *Rating by Manager* lines: one ("Reason for Leaving") shows the real reasons for the candidate leaving the two most recent jobs; and the other ("Rating by Manager") are the guesses as to how managers, in calls arranged by the candidate, will rate the candidate's overall performance.

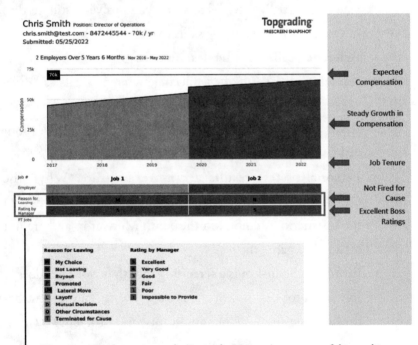

Note: *Pay special attention to the 'Rating by Manager' component of this graphic as it is a critical piece of information regarding a candidate's performance.*

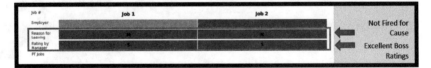

Here you see an applicant who is not a job hopper. He might be in your salary range (the top, black horizontal line), and he says he left jobs for reasons other than being fired. Most important, knowing he'll have to arrange reference calls with bosses, he has accurately guessed how those bosses would rate him. As you've learned, millions of reference calls have been made using this process, and clients agree that the applicants' guesses turn out to be very accurate. They know because they see what ratings candidates said they'd get and later confirm those ratings in calls with bosses.

The PreScreen Snapshot is simple to use. It's so intuitive that almost all free-trial users get started without any assistance. If you need a manual, a video, or live training, no problem. They're all available. If you'd like one-on-one help, call or schedule a call with our customer service team. We're happy to answer any questions or walk you through your setup. And the money-back guarantee is for real.

You might wonder, "Does the PreScreen Snapshot eliminate candidates?" No, it focuses your attention on the one-third who are most honest and highest performing. You still have the other résumés, but clients say that phone screening people who did not fill out the two-job questionnaire is a waste of time.

Use the QR code above to begin your PreScreen Snapshot free trial.

Chapter Summary

- There are many proven and effective ability, skill, knowledge, and interest tests.

- Some personality tests (Myers-Briggs, MMPI) are too often misused, and others do more harm than good, eliminating as many A Players as C Players.

- We've said that personality tests can be faked, so the results are suspect. Ironically, because the PreScreen Snapshot has the Truth Motivator in the Instructions, candidates filling out the PreScreen Snapshot form are probably honest ... and you can probably trust their personality test results.

- In recent years, there has been a flood of AI-assisted screening tools fraught with widespread problems.

- AI-assisted screening tools have the potential to be (1) fairer than conclusions by interviewers (who might harbor biases); (2) fairer than unstructured interviews (that have bias); (3) a great time-saver for recruiters (this already exists); (4) acceptable to candidates for these reasons; (5) inexpensive; and (6) effective (like the best employment tests).

- Although their marketing looks great and claims sound logical, AI-assisted screening tools are the most quoted cost-of-mishire form in the world.

- Past behavior (performance) is the best predictor of future behavior (performance); screening from résumés and application forms is typical and legally defensible.

- The PreScreen Snapshot is a two-job form that identifies the most honest, highest performing applicants. It does not suffer from the many proven flaws of most testing tools and applicant-screening instruments.

CHAPTER 9

Resources
(at https://topgrading.com/)

1. **Attend a virtual or live (in-person) two-day Topgrading workshop.** Take the best course to help you move from first aid to an EMT in hiring, maybe on your way to becoming a hiring brain surgeon. You learn all the Topgrading methods but also get personal coaching on your practice Tandem Topgrading interview.

   On-site Topgrading workshops are available when companies roll out Topgrading and want all managers trained.

2. **Read *Improve Your Hiring Process: Reach Peak Performance by Hiring Over 80% High Performers*, our latest eGuide.** Download it for free.

3. **Read Topgrading case studies.** Click on "Client Results" at https://topgrading.com/. You might be interested in taking a look at case studies to get advice from Topgraders.

- Access Development
- Amazon
- American Heart Association
- Argo Group
- Automation X
- Azura Memory Care
- Batesville
- Benco Dental
- Carestream Health
- Citadel
- Columbus McKinnon
- ConnXus
- Corwin Beverage Company
- Culligan
- DenTek
- DPT
- E*TRADE
- EMC
- General Electric
- ghSMART
- GSI
- Hayes Lemmerz
- HeimLantz
- Helpflow
- Hillenbrand
- Home Instead Senior Care
- K&N Management

- Labsphere
- LearnWell
- Lincoln Financial
- LLT, LLP
- Los Niños Services
- MarineMax
- Michael Schweitzer (Career)
- Mint.com (start-up, sold)
- Netsurit
- North American Nursing Education
- Nurse Next Door
- Onyx MD
- ProService Hawaii
- Red Door Interactive
- Roundy's
- Santa Teresa
- SIGMA Marketing
- Subserveo
- Synergia One
- TEKMORE
- TJ Johnson (Career)
- Triton
- Virtual Technology
- Wingman Coaching, LLC

4. **Use the Topgrading Cost of Bad Hire Calculator.** This is the most quoted mis-hire calculator, used by companies large and small to drive home the high costs of mis-hires in both money and time. It's free (https://topgrading.com/resources/mis-hire-calculator/).

5. **Consider professional Topgrading assessments of candidates for upper-level jobs.** Since the costs of mis-hires at senior levels are extremely high, CEOs and HR ask us to assess finalists for hire or promotion for those roles. This involves creating a job scorecard and conducting a four- to five-hour Topgrading interview, usually in tandem with the CEO or hiring manager. The client receives a detailed report with hire/no-hire recommendation, plus ratings and explanations of all key competencies. The new hire receives feedback and coaching from the Topgrading professional, plus a recommended individual development plan (approved by the CEO/HR in advance of the feedback meeting). Over 90 percent of the candidates we recommend turn out to be high performers.

    Here is a snapshot of what might have been a six-page report:

Pro's Assessment

Strengths

- Enthusiasm/Passion
- Resourcefulness/Initiative
- Accountability
- Selecting A players
- Judgment/Decision Making
- Redeploying B/C players
- Integrity
- Leading edge
- Track record
- Analysis skills
- Conceptual ability
- Pragmatism
- Education
- Experience
- Self-awareness
- Self-objectivity
- Written Communications
- Tenacity
- Highly Dependable
- Planning/Organization
- Listening
- Coaching

Weaker Areas

- Team player (at times good, but at other times needs to offer more opinions)
- Change Leadership (drives successful change, but could get more buy-in to have the change be quicker and better)
- Experience (fine for position applying for, but needs more business education for eventual general management)
- Stress management (regresses to introversion)
- Likability (generally very well liked, but initially a bit cold)

Topgrading.

6. **License Topgrading Online Solutions.** TOLS is our full software that is used when all the Topgrading methods are in place. TOLS integrates with applicant tracking systems.

7. **Ask a Topgrading professional to help you implement Topgrading.** This starts with understanding the company history and goals, current talent, plans for training managers, software setup, and plans to help the company perform the measurements that assure success. An initial step is to perform the measurements you read about—and be sure the company does these annually.

Annual Measurement

Hiring Success Rate	Undesirable Turnover	Promoting Success Rate	Current Team
When you hire someone from outside the company, what percent of the time does that person turn out to be an A Player?	What percentage of A Players are leaving the organization each year?	When you promote someone or move someone laterally in the organization, what percent of the time does that person turn out to be an A Player?	What percentage of your current team are A Players, A Potentials, and non-A Players?

Topgrading.

155

CHAPTER 10

Summary—Foolproof Hiring and the Future

The advice in this book can be summarized as the Topgrading Formula:

$$R + PSSS + TTM + TTI + RC$$

$$=$$

Career Success for Managers and Increased Company Profit

1. R = Recruit the Right Way

Topgrading means hiring the rare A Players from a large pool of applicants, so take whatever steps you must to maximize your applicant pool. Start by creating a job scorecard that clearly identifies the results you expect from your hire. Then tap the networks of your employees, friends, and associates, looking for candidates and referrals to candidates. Post your job on your "Careers" page and LinkedIn. Consider paying bonuses for employee referrals. And bite the bullet: use job boards to find both active and passive candidates. If necessary, increase pay and pay sign-on bonuses.

2. PSSS = Use the PreScreen Snapshot

Test-drive the screening tool that automatically ensures that all four major hiring problems are at least partially solved (Truth Motivator, revealing interviews, candidate-arranged reference calls, screening tool). It's free for as long as it takes to fill one job, up to three months. The PreScreen Snapshot is intuitive to set up and use. The two-job form is sent to all applicants, and you immediately see the best candidates, saving you time. You'll have two virtual piles of résumés: the one-third who filled out the form (focus on them) and the two-thirds who didn't (if you phone screen a couple, you'll find out their résumés were hyped).

3. TTM = Use the Topgrading Truth Motivator

Begin using the Topgrading Truth Motivator right away. Candidates who are forthcoming and sharp will be better performers and save you money by cutting screening costs in half.

As soon as you start using the Truth Motivator, you will finally, for the first time in your career, feel sure candidates are being open and honest.

4. TTI = Conduct Tandem Topgrading Interviews

Conduct at least a lite version of the Tandem Topgrading interview. You're probably overworked, behind in your hiring commitments, and the idea of taking a couple of hours for a chronological interview is daunting.

Yes, we know, but do it just once, and you'll be convinced that the Tandem Topgrading interview is by far the most revealing interview you can conduct. So you interview fewer but better candidates. And for every mis-hire you avoid, you save hundreds of hours that would have been spent dealing with their mistakes.

5. RC = Conduct Candidate-Arranged Reference Calls

It would be foolish not to after using the Truth Motivator. As you've learned, candidates get back to you and say when their bosses (and others) would be happy to talk to you. It's the best possible verification of what candidates told you. And did we mention? No phone tag!

After wasting time talking to friends of candidates, you'll know the candidate-arranged reference calls give you straight answers and useful insights on how to best manage new hires.

What You Can Expect—Short Term and Long Term

Improved company success. The ultimate "bottom line" is profits. By now you've probably gone to Topgrading.com, clicked on "Client Results," and read quotes from CEOs—such as "The company would have gone out of business if we hadn't Topgraded" (Paul Idzik, CEO of E*TRADE) or "With Topgrading I sold my start-up for $170 million" (Aaron Patzer, founder of Mint.com). These are glimpses of reality, not fantasy. We publish dozens of case studies, but there have been hundreds of other companies with similar results that could be cited too.

> The single biggest satisfaction we get is helping managers like you enjoy a more successful career.

Increased success for every hiring manager and human resources. The single biggest satisfaction we get is helping managers like you enjoy a more successful career. We very much appreciate the thank-you emails we get from not only CEOs (for more profits) but also managers at every level, who are more successful because they have many more high performers on their team—which assures better performance, more promotions, and less stress. If, as a hiring manager, you've lived with too many underperformers and the Top-grading methods in this book enable you to add just *one* more high performer and avoid just *one* poor performer, good for you. You're off to a great start. You didn't just read about the Topgrading keys, you but experienced getting the deeper, more thorough insights into candidates. So you will naturally commit to learning and practicing more, to make hiring high performers routine.

And if you're an HR manager, one unusually successful hire using Topgrading will convince you that honesty, thoroughness, and solid verification are keys to your success. Presenting fewer but better candidates to your internal clients, the hiring managers, will lead to them packing their teams with A Players, and you will be considered a rock star! The better you get, the more your internal clients will appreciate and respect you. And you will be at the top of your profession, a top 1 percent HR professional who has doubled or even tripled Quality of Hire.

Our hope is that almost all companies follow Culligan's lead in not just permitting but encouraging managers to take reference calls and to be totally candid—even explaining why an employee was fired for cause. Until then, don't settle for mediocre hiring methods—Topgrade!

This book was written to explain the simple key methods we briefly discuss in webinars and other basic Topgrading materials, so if we have missed something, something that makes you hesitate, please call or email us, and we'd be happy to talk, understand your situation, share our experience, and boost your confidence to stay with Topgrading keys.

Brad Smart   Chris Mursau